ONE WOMAN'S WEST

One Woman's West

The Life of Mary-Russell Ferrell Colton

by RICHARD K. AND SHERRY G. MANGUM

in cooperation with

MUSEUM OF NORTHERN ARIZONA

Northland Publishing

To my parents, H. Karl and Jessie Mae Mangum, Sine Qua Non.—R.K.M.

To my parents, Irving and Miriam Wiser.
My unending gratitude for introducing me, at a tender age,
to the beauty and peace of the Painted Desert.—S.G.M.

Text type was set in Fournier
Display type was set in Facade and Bank Gothic
Cover design by Rudy J. Ramos
Designed by Trina Stahl
Edited by Susan Tasaki
Editorial direction by Tom Carpenter
Production supervised by Lisa Brownfield
Composed and manufactured in the United States of America

FIRST EDITION
First softcover printing
ISBN 0-87358-613-1

Library of Congress Catalog Card Number
Mangum, Richard K.
One woman's West : the life of Mary-Russell Ferrell Colton / by
Richard K. and Sherry G. Mangum.
p.   cm.
"In cooperation with Museum of Northern Arizona."
Includes bibliographical references and index.
ISBN 0-87358-613-1 (sc)
1. Colton, Mary-Russell Ferrell, 1889– 2. Painters—United
States—Biography. 3. Southwest, New—In art. 4. Colton, Mary
Russell Ferrell, 1889– —Contributions in art patronage.
I. Mangum, Sherry G. II. Museum of Northern Arizona. III. Title.
ND237.C6743M36 1997
759.13—dc21
[B]   97-26830

0666/3.5M/8-97

Contents

ILLUSTRATIONS

Acknowledgments

WE ARE ESPECIALLY grateful to J. Ferrell Colton, Mary-Russell's son, for allowing us free access to the family archives at the Museum of Northern Arizona, some of which had previously been restricted. Ferrell also had us as guests in his home, where he graciously shared his recollections, photographs, paintings, and souvenirs.

We also thank the staff of the Museum of Northern Arizona, who were very helpful, particularly Michael Fox, Director, and Barbara Thurber, Librarian.

Thanks also to Katharine Bartlett, who shared her memories with us.

Mary-Russell Ferrell Colton Family Tree: Paternal Line

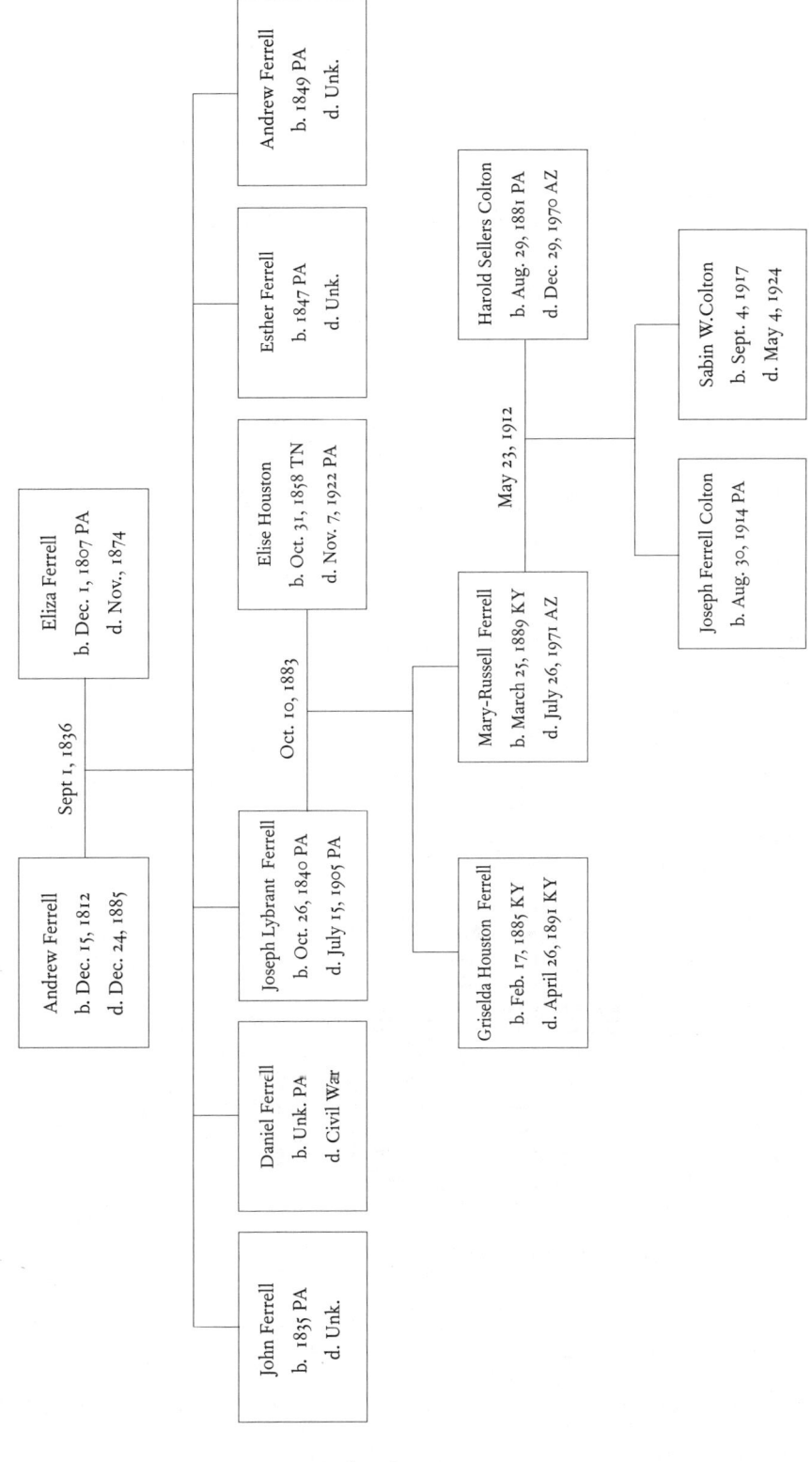

Andrew Ferrell
b. Dec. 15, 1812
d. Dec. 24, 1885

Sept 1, 1836

Eliza Ferrell
b. Dec. 1, 1807 PA
d. Nov., 1874

John Ferrell
b. 1835 PA
d. Unk.

Daniel Ferrell
b. Unk. PA
d. Civil War

Joseph Lybrant Ferrell
b. Oct. 26, 1840 PA
d. July 15, 1905 PA

Esther Ferrell
b. 1847 PA
d. Unk.

Andrew Ferrell
b. 1849 PA
d. Unk.

Oct. 10, 1883

Elise Houston
b. Oct. 31, 1858 TN
d. Nov. 7, 1922 PA

Griselda Houston Ferrell
b. Feb. 17, 1885 KY
d. April 26, 1891 KY

Mary-Russell Ferrell
b. March 25, 1889 KY
d. July 26, 1971 AZ

May 23, 1912

Harold Sellers Colton
b. Aug. 29, 1881 PA
d. Dec. 29, 1970 AZ

Joseph Ferrell Colton
b. Aug. 30, 1914 PA

Sabin W. Colton
b. Sept. 4, 1917
d. May 4, 1924

Mary-Russell Ferrell Colton Family Tree: Maternal Line

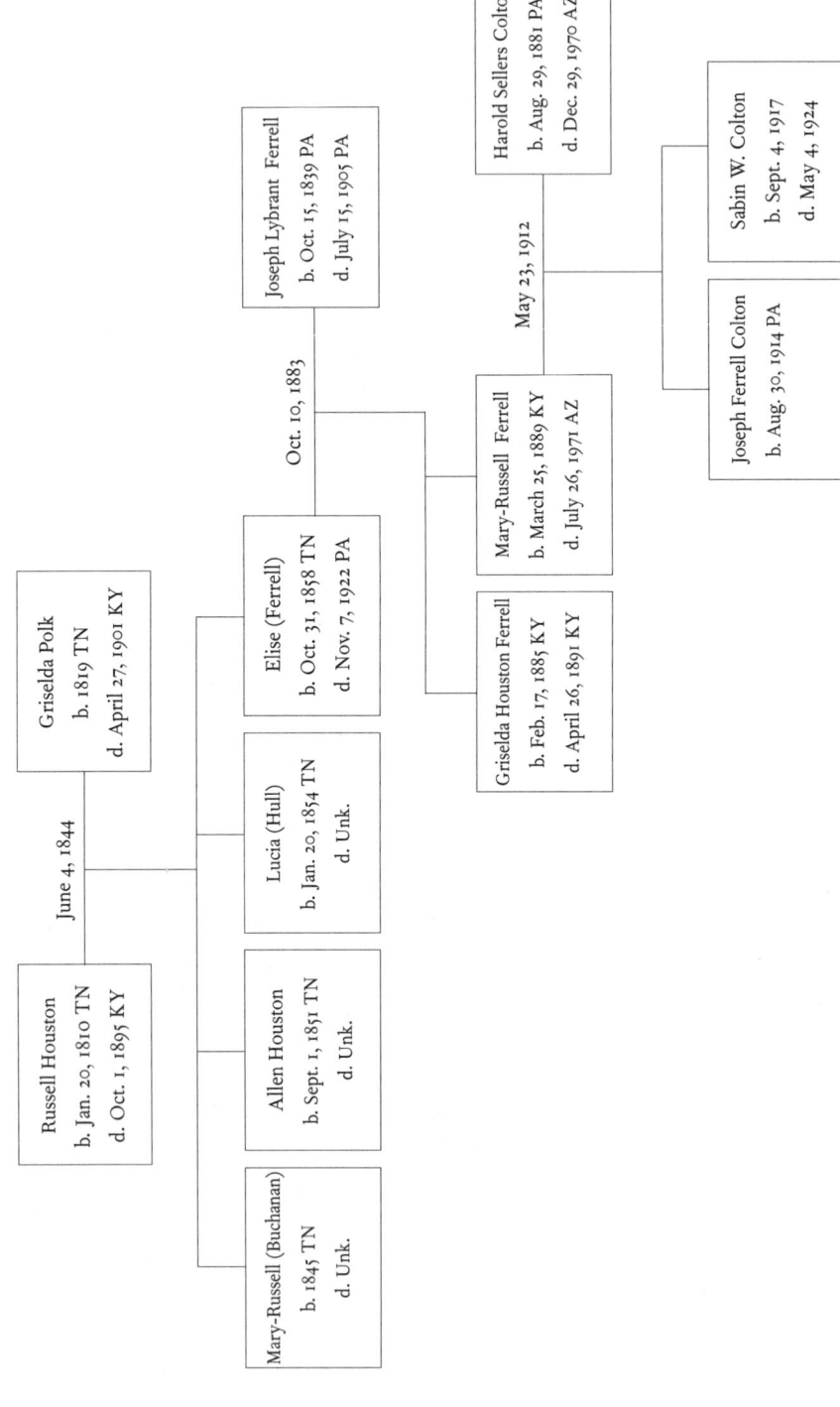

Russell Houston
b. Jan. 20, 1810 TN
d. Oct. 1, 1895 KY

Griselda Polk
b. 1819 TN
d. April 27, 1901 KY

June 4, 1844

Joseph Lybrant Ferrell
b. Oct. 15, 1839 PA
d. July 15, 1905 PA

Harold Sellers Colton
b. Aug. 29, 1881 PA
d. Dec. 29, 1970 AZ

Mary-Russell (Buchanan)
b. 1845 TN
d. Unk.

Allen Houston
b. Sept. 1, 1851 TN
d. Unk.

Lucia (Hull)
b. Jan. 20, 1854 TN
d. Unk.

Elise (Ferrell)
b. Oct. 31, 1858 TN
d. Nov. 7, 1922 PA

Oct. 10, 1883

Griselda Houston Ferrell
b. Feb. 17, 1885 KY
d. April 26, 1891 KY

Mary-Russell Ferrell
b. March 25, 1889 KY
d. July 26, 1971 AZ

May 23, 1912

Joseph Ferrell Colton
b. Aug. 30, 1914 PA

Sabin W. Colton
b. Sept. 4, 1917
d. May 4, 1924

ANDREW FERRELL,
MARY-RUSSELL'S PATERNAL
GRANDFATHER, CIRCA 1870

ELIZA FERRELL, MARY-
RUSSELL'S PATERNAL
GRANDMOTHER, CIRCA 1870

JOSEPH FERRELL,
MARY-RUSSELL'S FATHER,
CIRCA 1880

ELISE HOUSTON FERRELL,
MARY-RUSSELL'S MOTHER, WITH
INFANT MARY-RUSSELL, 1889

JUDGE RUSSELL HOUSTON,
MARY-RUSSELL'S PATERNAL
GRANDFATHER, HOLDING
MARY-RUSSELL, 1891

GRISELDA POLK HOUSTON,
MARY-RUSSELL'S MATERNAL
GRANDMOTHER, 1892

Introduction

MARY-RUSSELL FERRELL COLTON was born in 1889 into a fast-changing world. A natural artist, her talent was recognized early and was nurtured by family and friends. Study at the Philadelphia School of Design for Women focused her skills and reinforced her conviction that art was an essential part of life.

Raised in Philadelphia in a tradition that, similar to the horse and buggy, has now all but disappeared, she was also trained to be a lady. She was taught that those who had money had a moral responsibility to share it with those who did not, and that she should try to make the world a better place for having lived in it. Throughout her life, Mary-Russell practiced these beliefs with complete integrity.

As a young woman, she had an opportunity to explore the West in the summers of 1909 and 1910. Before the second trip, she met (and later wed) Harold S. Colton, a fellow Philadelphian and a scientist who was then teaching zoology at the University of Pennsylvania. Married in 1912, the Coltons kept their summers free and spent many of their vacations in the West, even after two children came into their lives. The couple roamed throughout the Southwest when the area was still largely unspoiled, exploring it on horseback, by wagon, and with various eccentric motor-powered vehicles. During their travels, they discovered Flagstaff, Arizona; they spent several summers there before deciding, in 1926, to pull up their deep Eastern roots and move to Flagstaff permanently.

Mary-Russell was determined to bring art to this still-pioneer region of northern Arizona, and successfully did so. Children in the public schools and townspeople alike benefited from her enthusiasm and talent. Further, she dedicated herself to reviving Hopi and Navajo craft art, which was then being replaced by machine-made goods and curios attractive to tourists.

The Coltons led the founding of the Museum of Northern Arizona in 1928, and the institution not only became a home for Mary-Russell's ideas but also provided a framework within which to carry them out. Through the museum, she created an ambitious, multifaceted program that included teaching art, exhibiting fine art to the people of the region, and reviving Indian art. She devoted her energy, her money, and her talent to this agenda for the rest of her life.

A devout champion of the Hopis, she spoke on their behalf in public causes and was their friend, counselor, broker, and errand-runner. She preserved knowledge of their folklore and ways. If any one person can be given credit for saving Hopi arts and crafts from extinction, it would have to be Mary-Russell. She created, organized, and nurtured the Hopi Craftsman Exhibition so effectively that it became the pre-eminent Indian arts and crafts show in the nation. Modern Hopi silver owes its existence to Mary-Russell, and the craft of Hopi potterymaking was, to a great degree, restored by her study of coloring agents and firing methods. Hopi dyes were brought back from oblivion through her diligence, and the Hopis' beautiful traditional woven goods were saved from slipping into garish and shoddy shadows of themselves by her efforts to obtain natural materials such as indigo, cochineal, madder, long staple cotton, and suitable wool for the weavers.

A prolific and gifted writer, she produced twenty-one published articles and the authoritative book, *Hopi Dyes.*

As a teacher, she contributed best by writing a classic book on art education for school children, *Art for the Schools of the Southwest.* She invented the Treasure Chest program and the Junior Art Show, and hosted numerous exhibitions of high-quality art over the years at the Museum of Northern Arizona to set an example.

Mary-Russell Ferrell Colton's many gifts of land and other valuable property to the Museum of Northern Arizona were instrumental in ensuring the viability and success of that institution. From its earliest days, the museum was the beneficiary of her tireless efforts, which included organizing, promoting, and judging several exhibitions each year and donating prize money for most of them. Ultimately, she became known as one of the country's leading experts on Indian arts and crafts.

Late in life, she received a Citation of Merit from the United States Indian Arts and Crafts Board for her services, and was elected posthumously as a charter member of the Arizona Women's Hall of Fame. In spite of this recognition, her story is little known. We hope to remedy that with this book.

Chapter One

EARLY YEARS

MARY-RUSSELL FERRELL COLTON made her mark on the world in the West. But it was in the East that her story began.

Her father, Joseph Ferrell (born 1840), descended from a long line of Pennsylvania farmers. He attended Yale for a time; poor health caused him to leave school but did not prevent him from serving as paymaster in the Union navy during the Civil War. Following military service, he traveled extensively, going westward across the United States and then to the Far East. Once his travels were over, he located in Philadelphia, where he set up an engineering practice.

Mary-Russell's mother was Elise Houston, daughter of Judge Russell Houston, Chief Justice of the Supreme Court of Tennessee and later the president of the Louisville and Nashville Railroad. Elise's mother was a member of the famous Polk family of Tennessee.

Elise Houston and Joseph Ferrell met in Louisville when Ferrell went there at Russell Houston's invitation to engineer bridges for the railroad. In 1883, Joseph Ferrell and Elise Houston were married and set up housekeeping in Philadelphia in a wing of an old house owned by the widow Hamlin (called "Aunt Budgie" by the Ferrells), who occupied the rest of the home. The Ferrells had their first child, Griselda, on February 17, 1885. Their second and last child, Mary-Russell, was born at the Houston home in Louisville on

March 25, 1889, when Joseph Ferrell was almost fifty years old. On April 26, 1891, when Mary-Russell was only two, her sister Griselda died of diphtheria.

Joseph Ferrell left the management of the home to Aunt Budgie, whom Mary-Russell recalled was "a grand dame, who dressed in black bombazine and ruled the household." Aunt Budgie had two servants, a maid and a cook, who waited on the Ferrells as well as herself. The Ferrells had a governess, Julia McMahan, nicknamed "Dysie," hired when Griselda was born.

Mary-Russell remembered her father as a kind-hearted man with sparkling gray eyes. His hair and beard, auburn in his youth, were gray by the time Mary-Russell was born. He loved to tell Mary-Russell stories of his travels and adventures as a young man, and she listened to him spellbound.

ALTHOUGH MARY-RUSSELL had few playmates, her favorite companion was a neighbor boy named Parker Chase. She preferred his company to that of girls, she said, because he was "good at building things." Early in her life, this solitary child developed what was to become a lifelong response to conflict: if a situation or a person seemed troublesome, she avoided confrontation by withdrawing. Mary-Russell was never spanked for misbehaving; her punishment was generally to be confined to a chair, which the lively and energetic girl dreaded. It is to be imagined that Mary-Russell's parents had few occasions to punish her, however.

Mary-Russell demonstrated artistic talent at an early age, and was encouraged and praised for her work. The Christmas presents she most enjoyed receiving were paints and books, and with these, she was content to sit quietly, sketching or reading.

JOSEPH FERRELL LEFT engineering in 1886 to develop Broadwater Island off the coast of Virginia as a resort for wealthy Philadelphians. He built a clubhouse on the island, as well as a cottage for his family. He also built a shelter on the mainland where visitors could wait for the ferry that carried them to and from Broadwater.

Broadwater Island's reputation was widespread. In 1892, when president-elect Grover Cleveland disappeared for a brief respite away from the public eye, he came secretly to the island for some hunting and fishing. Mary-Russell met him there, and one of her treasured memories was that of sitting on Cleveland's lap. She remembered him as a "nice jolly fat man."

Broadwater Island had a wide sandy beach, a few meadows, and a pine forest. The Ferrell family spent most of its summers there and Mary-Russell came to love it, calling it "my childhood paradise." Her hair in bangs and often barefoot, she explored the island on the back of a Chincoteague pony; a black servant named Ben Upshur went along to take care of her. She also

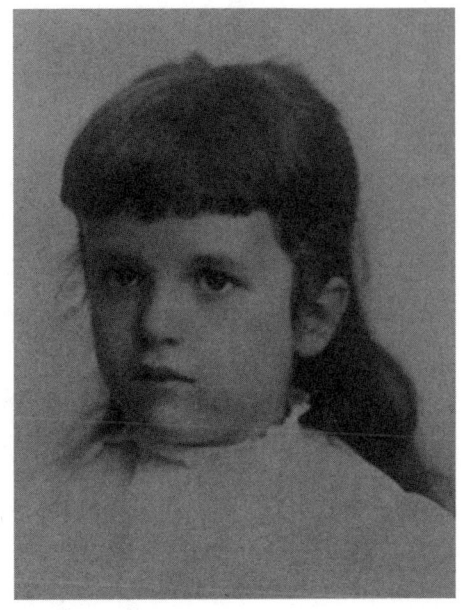

MARY-RUSSELL, AGE 6, 1895

learned how to fish, and came to love it. In fishing as in every other activity, she preferred to be alone; when she was still quite small, her parents tied a rope around her waist and anchored it to a bollard, which enabled her to spend solitary hours safely fishing off the Broadwater pier. She also enjoyed hiking around the island with her dogs. She loved animals and in addition to the dogs, had lambs, geese, and chickens; the latter followed her around as though they were domesticated pets.

Those childhood summers not spent on Broadwater were passed with her relatives in Louisville. These (in addition to Grandmother and Grandfather Houston) included her mother's sister Mary-Russell Buchanan (Mary Russell Ferrell's namesake) and her husband Lytle (whom Mary-Russell called "Unkie").

MARY-RUSSELL RECEIVED her early education at home. Lessons in piano and the mandolin were part of the curriculum, though she never became proficient on either instrument. Her formal schooling began when she was eight and started attending Pelham Academy, a private school for girls. Although some scholarly subjects were in the curriculum, the real aim of Pelham Academy was to teach its students how to be ladies. As an adult, Mary-Russell described her education:

The Misses McMurtrie ran the Pelham School on Pelham Road. [My] formal education was most casual by today's standards. [I] lived in a literary atmosphere. [My father] taught [me] mathematics. [I] learned to read at an early age. History was taught by [my] mother, while [my] Aunt taught composition. Grammar was natural and spelling was never taught formally. [I] left Pelham school before graduation so never had a formal diploma. [I] was always surrounded by cultured, scientific, and literary people, both relatives and friends.

Although her schooling may have been casual, Mary-Russell enjoyed education. She had a great ability to learn and a lively, inquiring mind, and these enabled her to absorb a great deal from reading, conversations, and other sources. Later in life, she astonished visiting scientists with the depth of her knowledge over a wide range of subjects.

MARY-RUSSELL, AGE 11, 1900

Mary-Russell also took art lessons. A letter she wrote to her father (undated, but probably composed when she was eight) reads,

Dear Papa, I have taken 9 painting lessons, from Miss Sophie Gray Mrs. Berry sister, she is a lovely lady, and she paints beautiful pictures, and she has three others in her class besides me. Unkie is giving me these lessons, and I take them every other day, and I injoy them very much. And I want to know if you won't let me take some more lessons, won't you write as soon as you can and tell me if I can or not.

By the end of childhood, Mary-Russell wanted two things out of life. One was to travel to faraway places. The other was to become an artist.

EVEN THOUGH JOSEPH FERRELL's Broadwater Island project was successful, it did not produce significant income, and increasingly, he concentrated on his first love, inventing. In the 1890s, he created a product that was to occupy the balance of his life: a fire-retardant solution. Wood dipped in this liquid became virtually fireproof. Hard at work developing the solution, he visited Broadwater less and less. This provoked the members to take control (and income) from him.

After he lost Broadwater, Ferrell worked exclusively on the fire retardant. The invention was a legitimate and worthwhile product, one which was granted a patent and awarded the Elliot Cresson medal of the Franklin Institute of Philadelphia. It was not, however, a commercial success.

Just as Mary-Russell was poised to begin academic art training, disaster befell the family when Joseph Ferrell's finances and health both failed. According to a family story, a friend and partner in the fire retardant project left, taking the formula with him. The treachery broke Ferrell's heart and led to his death. Nursed at home for several weeks until the end came, Joseph Ferrell died on July 15, 1904, at age sixty-four, when Mary-Russell was fifteen years old.

Upon her father's death, Mary-Russell and her mother immediately found themselves in straitened circumstances. Elise had to sell the family furniture, the cottage on Broadwater Island, and other valuable assets to cover their living expenses. When she became aware that there was no money to pay for

MARY-RUSSELL, AGE 15 (BACK ROW, RIGHT) WITH HER
CLASSMATES IN ART SCHOOL, 1904

academy training for Mary-Russell, a friend of the family, Mrs. Anne E.
Walbridge, came to the rescue by providing tuition for Mary-Russell's education at the Philadelphia School of Design for Women. One of the finest
art schools in the country, it billed itself as America's oldest college of art
for women.

With Mrs. Walbridge's money in hand, Mary-Russell applied for admission on October 11, 1904, less than three months after her father's death, and
was admitted on November 1, 1904. Admission to the prestigious school was
an honor, one that a student had to earn by displaying art works that showed
sufficient talent to justify enrollment. The classes were small and the training
intensive.

Joseph Ferrell's death also resulted in the breakup of the Hamlin home.
When Aunt Budgie sold the house and moved into a nursing home in Bethle-
hem, Pennsylvania, Mary-Russell and her mother also had to move. In July

1905, they relocated to Strousburg (another Philadelphia district), where they lived in a boarding house. From there, Mary-Russell commuted to art school by trolley, requiring a four-block walk and an hour's ride.

At fifteen, Mary-Russell was the youngest student in her class, but was serious about her studies, and gifted. Two of her teachers were well known, Elliott Daingerfield and Henry B. Snell, both of whom influenced her work.

She enjoyed art school. On January 5, 1906, she referred to herself in the third person in a letter to "Bug" (Ethel Whiteside, the nurse who tended Joseph Ferrell in his final illness and later became Mary-Russell's close friend):

> *Mary talks about being in the social whirl. She is studying French, Russian history and English Literature. She is also painting. For Christmas she received two books, one on art, the other was* Pony Tracks *by Remington, but it can't come up to* The Virginian *my old stand by.*

Although Mary-Russell may have described herself as being in the social whirl, by conventional standards she led a sheltered and private life. She seemed to have little interest in dances, games, and parties.

This lack of interest may have been partially a result of her self-imposed schedule. In spite of her long commute, she trained herself to get up early so that she could start work as soon as school opened in the morning. She applied herself all day and often stayed after-hours doing additional work. Such diligent students are sometimes disliked by less-energetic peers, but Mary-Russell's classmates are reported to have loved her, and many remained her close friends for life. Serious but not solemn, she radiated a quiet *joie de vivre*.

ONE OF THE annual projects given to the students at the Philadelphia School of Design was to create calendar illustrations. The calendar companies designated the themes but left it to the students to produce suitable paintings. This Mary-Russell enjoyed, as it provided considerable artistic latitude over a variety of subjects. It also gave her and her fellow students opportunities for fascinating and inexpensive shopping forays as they searched for props in second-hand stores. During this time, she learned how to restore and clean old paintings, and became known for her skill at this painstaking and delicate work.

In 1907, Mary-Russell won the P. Pemberton Morris scholarship, the funds from which paid for an additional year at the school, which was based on a three-year term.

By the time Mary-Russell entered her fourth year of training, she had blossomed into a beautiful young woman. Her striking looks were unaugmented by cosmetics; she never in her life wore any, thinking them improper for a decent woman. (On Mary-Russell's wedding day, Bug tried to get her to use a little rouge on her cheeks but she refused even that.) And though only five feet, two inches tall, she also disdained high heels.

During these art-school years, Mary-Russell made time to attend plays, symphonies, and operas. Philadelphia was then one of the leading centers of the American theater, and the greats of the day performed there. Among her souvenirs are programs indicating that she saw Sarah Bernhardt in *Camille*, 1906; Maud Adams in *Peter Pan*, 1907; Ethel Barrymore in *Her Sister*, 1907; and in 1908, Nazimova in *Hedda Gabler* and Isadora Duncan in a dance recital. She also saw a production of *Tosca*, starring Caruso and Scotti.

Absent from her keepsakes, however, is any indication of dating. It could be that she put aside extraneous emotional relationships for the sake of art. For Mary-Russell, art was neither a passing fancy nor a romantic indulgence. She believed that art should be part of all aspects of life, and that she should live for it. She was completely serious about this. Her Uncle Lytle described her as "a woman so wedded to her profession as to put aside all sentiment of love as interfering with her life's ambition."

In 1908, while Mary-Russell was still in art school, her mother remarried, which came as a great shock to the girl. Her mother's choice was Theodore Presser, a man well known in music circles as owner of the Presser Music Publishing House, the leading classical music press of the day, and publisher of *Etude*, America's premier magazine for musicians. The Presser home had been next door to the Ferrell-Hamlin home, and Elise had been a close friend of Presser's first wife, who died in 1905. Presser stayed in contact with Elise after she moved following Joseph Ferrell's death, eventually began a courtship, and proposed marriage. Dysie followed Elise and became a servant in the Presser home. With this marriage came an infusion of wealth into the family. However, even though Presser bought Mary-Russell fine things, including an elegant wardrobe, relations between the two were strained.

WHEN MARY-RUSSELL finished her undergraduate term and received her diploma in May 1908, she was awarded the John Sartain Post-Graduate scholarship. This enabled her to have a fifth year of study, which would begin at the end of a summer spent at a girls' camp in Maine. Although Mary-Russell was certainly past the age to be sent away to camp, her mother seems to have felt that the situation at home was too tense for Mary-Russell to stay there during the vacation.

After Mary-Russell finished her post-graduate work in May 1909, she set up a little art studio in downtown Philadelphia. She continued to live in the Presser home, and now, her commute was to work rather than school. She had as partners in the studio two class-mates, Helen McCarthy and Lucille Howard. Lucille later went her own way and Mary-Russell and Helen moved to a different studio.

Although Mary-Russell was trained to work in pencil, ink,

THEODORE AND ELISE PRESSER
(MARY-RUSSELL'S STEPFATHER
AND MOTHER), 1908

charcoal, watercolor, sculpture, and carving, she preferred doing landscapes in oil. Since it was difficult to make a living selling original works of fine art, she augmented her income with restoration work, which she performed for both individuals and museums. She and Helen were able to eke out livings in this fashion.

Apparently, the friction between Mary-Russell and her stepfather continued after she graduated, and her mother thought it would be a good idea to get her out of the house again in the summer of 1909. She mentioned the situation to her friends, including Aunt Budgie. The latter was a friend of physician Jane Myers, whom Budgie called "Dr. Jane." Dr. Jane, in turn, was a friend of Dr. Charles Shaw, a faculty member of the University of Pennsylvania. Shaw, a botanist, was fascinated by the Selkirk Mountains of British Columbia and had made several summer expeditions there. He frequently took students with him on these trips, and had a few openings for the 1909 excursion. Dr. Jane

FIRST SELKIRK TRIP. MARY-RUSSELL IN REVELSTOKE, B. C., 1909

mentioned this trip to Aunt Budgie, who thought it might be just what Elise was looking for.

The suggestion to go to the Selkirks with Shaw was made to Mary-Russell and she accepted the notion eagerly, even though it would be a complete departure from anything the sheltered city girl had ever done before. Perhaps her late father's stories about trekking in the American West predisposed her to try it. When the trip began, Mary-Russell traveled to the Canadian rendezvous by herself. En route, she wrote her mother that even though this was the first trip she had ever taken alone, "I enjoy very much managing for myself and find that I am well able to do it, and not having a reckless disposition I get into no trouble, so don't worry."

The Shaw expedition—six students and two adults—assembled at Rogers Pass, British Columbia, on the Fourth of July. Mary-Russell described each of them to her mother by their nicknames: Rosy, Yellow Kid, Pittie, Bub, Sunny Jim, Jamie, and Skipper, adding, "We are such a happy family just like brothers & sisters. The men are all such perfect gentlemen, though each is so different." Mary-Russell's nickname, "Fairy," was provided by Blanche Shaw, wife of Charles "Skipper" Shaw.

Once the party mustered, they got underway and had hardly a moment of spare time thereafter. On July 23, 1909, Mary-Russell found a little break in the group's hectic activities and used it to write to her mother:

It seems as though I had been here years, we have done so much & know everybody so well.

On Tuesday we went on a long hike up Grizzly Mt., as I told you, Wednesday a hike up the snow sheds & sketching. Thursday the greatest time of my life, we climbed Ursus Minor, not quite reaching the top on account of a storm . . . never hoped to have such fun in my life, am in camp today.

I must tell you how we went coasting in July. On the way down yesterday we decided to come down in a hurry and coming to a great snow slide which went almost straight down and disappeared over a curving edge the Dr. said let's take the elevator & with that he sat down held his legs up & shot down some thousand ft. out of sight; one by one with a shout down we went, landing in the Dr.'s arms in a flurry of snow. And so we proceeded downwards for several thousand ft., till out of the snow fields, sometimes all seven of us at once, holding on to each other's feet. I never hoped to have such fun in my life, and all the time too you are roasting up there in the snow. (This tobogganing without a toboggan is called glissading).

The Dr. is so fine & good, I think he is the finest character I have ever known. He takes care of us like his own little children. He is always doing something for somebody else. . . . There are only 9 in camp & every one jolly and fine. They call me Fairy and pet me to death. Am so happy but want you and Daddy P. to see this country.

After hiking in the Rogers Pass area, the party went by train to Revelstoke, where they took a steamer up the Columbia River, against the south-flowing current. In places, the crew had to use ropes to pull the vessel over rapids. Leaving the boat after three days, they began working their way into the back country, first with horses, then on foot. Mary-Russell confided to her mother that she was hiking in bloomers, something the ladies at Pelham Academy would no doubt have found improper.

In two days, they reached the Standard Cabin, which had been used as a base for a copper-mining operation a few years earlier. The cabin was fully stocked with canned goods and they used it for several days. Mary-Russell reported that, "I didn't get my clothes off but once in 2 weeks."

Mountains covered with snow banks surrounded the cabin, and the hikers again took up the sport of glissading, this time with unpleasant results: Mary-Russell broke a rib. Knowing that her mother would fret when she learned of the injury, she wrote soon afterwards that she was not only in good spirits and good health but that she was "a new woman living a new life."

When the expedition broke up at the end of the summer, Mary-Russell came home via Yellowstone National Park, which she reached on September 13, 1909. She spent a few days there sightseeing and then returned to Philadelphia in late September, greatly refreshed in spirit. She now had a new love in her life: the American West.

But art was still most important. She went back to work, commuting from the Presser home to her downtown art studio, which she continued to operate with her partner Helen McCarthy. Aunt Budgie wrote to her that October, commenting upon the Selkirk trip and Mary-Russell's activities since her return:

I cannot help thinking constantly how your father would have sympathized in every moment of your experiences and entirely approved of your surroundings. And now for the studio—and the work to be done in it. I don't wonder you say you are crazy to get at the work!

IN MAY 1910, Dr. Charles Shaw decided to host another trip to the Selkirks, and held a meeting for those who had been on the 1909 trip as well as interested newcomers. The 1910 expedition was to be the longest and toughest Shaw had led, and was ultimately his last.

Mary-Russell attended the gathering and there met Harold S. Colton, an instructor in zoology at the University of Pennsylvania. Colton's friend, Dr. Merkle H. "Ben" Jacobs, had been on several Selkirk outings and was to be the second-in-command in 1910. Colton, who usually spent his summers sailing his yacht *Clione*, was prevailed upon by Jacobs to join the 1910 expedition. Shaw asked Mary-Russell to evaluate Colton to see whether he was suitable. She approved him, though neither was especially impressed by the other at the time. Harold later wrote, "I reported to my mother on the party. . . . and the people that I met. On describing Fairy, I reported that she had little style."

The goal of the 1910 trip was to go up the Columbia River from Revelstoke, around the Big Bend, and then back down to the railroad at Donald. This meant traveling forty miles by

SECOND SELKIRK TRIP.
HAROLD S. COLTON AND
MARY-RUSSELL, 1910

steamer, another forty-five miles by pack train, and a final ninety-five miles by foot.

Dr. Shaw recommended that the participants do some sightseeing after the expedition was completed. Mary-Russell and several others followed his advice, and made plans to travel through the western United States at the conclusion of the activities in Canada. Their itinerary was to take the Canadian Pacific Railroad to Vancouver, then go south on American railroads to Los Angeles, finally taking the Santa Fe through the Southwest. In Chicago, they would connect with the Pennsylvania Railroad for the return home.

En route to the starting point, Mary-Russell took a side trip to Waterloo, Iowa, to visit Blanche Shaw at her parents' home. Then, accompanied by Blanche and her children—Harland, six, and baby Gretchen—she traveled by rail to British Columbia.

The party met at Rogers Pass, again on the Fourth of July. Harold wrote his mother: "There we met Mrs. Shaw, the children, and Miss Ferrell who looked as if she belonged to the Wild West. . . . She is the only picturesque one of the bunch."

Mary-Russell noticed Harold too. She wrote her mother, "Dr. Coulton [sic] . . . is with us and a very nice man." The group consisted of three adult males: Shaw, Jacobs, and Colton; a sixteen-year old boy nicknamed Son; Shaw's son, Harland, six; and five women. Two of the women, Yellow Kid and Lorelei, were slightly older than Mary-Russell, while the other two, Granny Lu and The Missionary, were much older.

They traveled to Revelstoke by railroad and boarded a steamer headed up the Columbia River. Leaving the boat on July 10, the party hiked into the back country, up the LaForme River Valley to Standard Cabin. Mary-Russell seemed to thrive on the hardships, even the bad weather that hit the party.

In a letter to her mother, Mary-Russell confided:

I write to you this way because you are my mother, and with my heart I pray you to understand, because I love you so. These great moods of nature move my very soul, and though I love her when she smiles, it is the wild dark mood, the shrieking wind and flying snow that seem to lift me up and bear me on with the storm on the wings of freedom.

Do not laugh, I am giving you myself, trying to have you understand, and all the time my faith in God is strengthened.

After a stay of several days, the group hiked back to the river and took the steamer to the end of the line. Disembarking at LaPorte, they picked up a string of pack horses and hiked north, reaching Mica Creek Cabin on July 23; they left the horses at this point. From Mica Creek, they continued on foot to the Big Bend, reaching it on July 26. Two men, Markensen and Crawford, ran a ferry there, and were astonished to see the group, especially the women. The ferry cable had been broken by the thaw-swollen river, so the ferrymen rowed the expeditioners across the Columbia in a small boat. It took three trips to get them all to the east shore.

Shaw's party had been told that Kinbasket Lake, their next stop, was thirty-five miles from the point to which they had been rowed. After a brief hike, they rested overnight. The next day, Shaw pushed the hikers very hard, almost exhausting the older women before making camp. The following morning, figuring that Kinbasket was still a hard day's hike down the trail, Harold and Ben, the strongest walkers, set out at dawn to get to a previously cached canoe and use it to find a camping place. To their surprise, they reached the lake an hour after setting out. Kinbasket was not nearly as far away as they had been told. Locating a good camp site across the lake, the two returned to find everyone waiting for them. The men then made several canoe trips to take everyone to the campsite.

After two days at Lake Kinbasket, Colton and Jacobs left the expedition, Colton to do marine biology work at the Scripps Institute in La Jolla, California, and Jacobs to join his fiancée in Georgia. Mary-Russell wrote a letter to her mother on July 29, 1910, and gave it to Harold to post for her.

Tomorrow, Ben and Dr. Coulton start out, hence the letter, but we will remain as long as the grub lasts, the 10th [of August] being the latest to strike the railroad.

Kinbasket is more beautiful than the imagination, seven miles long and two miles wide, on one side of the Selkirks dark shadows rise precipitous from the deep mirror surface of the lake, on the other rise the ragged bare peaks of the Rockies, forbidding and snowless against the sky.

Since we crossed the Columbia two days ago at the Bend, we have been in

*the Rockies and are now camped on a pebbly beach on the shore near the torrent
fan of Middle River; we look across through a V-shaped notch up to a mighty
trident shaped snow capped peak and a mighty hanging glacier, fed by the snows
above, and to right and left the great snow heads appear above the forested
slopes.*

On July 30, Shaw rowed Jacobs and Colton down the lake, past the
mouths of three rivers, to a point where they could take a southbound trail. As
they parted, Harold noted that Shaw was sitting far back in the canoe, which
caused the tip to stick up out of the water, and was concerned about the
botanist's safety.

The little group at Lake Kinbasket waited in vain for Shaw to return. After
several hours had passed, they feared that something was wrong and decided
to get help. Mary-Russell, Yellow Kid, and Son, the best hikers, tried to hike
to the south but were blocked by the Middle River, which almost swept them
away when they attempted to cross it. Realizing that they could not get out to
the south, they decided to go back to Big Bend.

The next morning, July 31, the three drew lots to determine who would go
and who would stay behind in charge of the camp. Mary-Russell got the short
straw. Yellow Kid and Son took to the trail, expecting to spend a night en route
before reaching Markensen and Crawford the following day. This left Mary-
Russell, Harland Shaw, Granny Lu, Lorelei, and The Missionary at Lake Kinbasket. The adults concealed the implications of what was happening from
Harland.

Yellow Kid and Son were successful and on August 2, reappeared with
Markensen and Crawford on a raft. Further help came unexpectedly when two
prospectors happened by in a canoe. The men mounted a search for Dr.
Shaw, but found only his upturned canoe. Eventually Mary-Russell's party
was boated to the southbound trail, and walked fifty miles to safety at Beavermouth, from where Mary-Russell sent a telegram to her mother, advising of
the tragedy.

Although Mary-Russell and her friends were rescued, an awful job lay
ahead, the ordeal of informing Blanche Shaw of her husband's death. Mrs.
Shaw was staying at Revelstoke with baby Gretchen and did not know what

had happened. Mary-Russell volunteered to take the news to Blanche, later regarding the task of informing Blanche of her husband's disappearance and trying to comfort her as one of the hardest things she ever had to do in her life. Blanche wanted to go to Lake Kinbasket to see the scene for herself, and Mary-Russell accompanied her, returning after several days to Beavermouth.

When they received Mary-Russell's news, her mother and step-father naturally worried. Assuming that Mary-Russell would collapse under the strain of such hardships and would want to return home immediately, they wired travel money. Mary-Russell was much stronger and braver than her mother and stepfather thought, however. She replied that she wanted to stick with the original plan and travel through the West.

Her parents yielded to her wishes, and Yellow Kid, Lorelei, Son, and Mary-Russell set off by train. They went to Vancouver, then visited Victoria, where Yellow Kid left. The remaining three then traveled on south to Seattle, Portland, and San Francisco.

During the long hours on the train, Mary-Russell thought deeply about what had happened. She reached out to her stepfather and wrote a conciliatory letter, asking that they be friends. She also wrote:

> *The wilderness of which you have such a horror holds no terrors for me, no, not even now. It beckons, beckons and claims its own, that is all, and if it is God's will, I will go back again, sometime but not next year. But the city and the places that are old with man shall never hold me. I must breathe.*

The trio arrived in Los Angeles at the end of August, where Harold Colton rejoined them. As Harold wrote to his mother,

> *Now I am personal conductor of the party of two females and the youth. . . . I really wondered what the crowd would look like as swell loafers. Fairy whom I had only twice seen attired in anything but a boy's flannel shirt and bloomers, did not disappoint me. She is just as cute in skirts.*

The foursome headed east on the Santa Fe railroad. On Tuesday, September 6, they arrived at the south rim of the Grand Canyon, where they had tea at the rim and camped overnight. The next day, they hiked below the rim to Indian Gardens, and then, after a rest, on down to the Colorado River. They returned the same day to Indian Gardens and spent the night, hiking back up to the top on September 8. They then rented horses and rode to Desert View, camping overnight. The travelers left the Grand Canyon by train, heading east. At Adamana, the station for the Petrified Forest, Harold stayed aboard while the rest of the party got off and spent two days sight-seeing. By late September, both Harold and Mary-Russell were back in Philadelphia, where he resumed his job teaching zoology at the University of Pennsylvania and she returned to her art career.

THE EVENTS OF the summer changed Mary-Russell's life, maturing her, making her self-reliant, giving her an abiding love for the Southwest, and introducing her to the man she would marry.

Chapter Two

Courtship, Marriage, and Motherhood

HAROLD HAD FALLEN in love with Mary-Russell. An attractive man, quick-witted, humorous, and generous, he was interested in everything and delighted in sharing his knowledge. Although he could seem a bit stiff and reserved, he had an impish sense of humor that gave him considerable charm. His personal circumstance of being both wealthy and well connected allowed him to work without salary. This was not an uncommon situation at the University of Pennsylvania at the time, where the faculty resembled a gentlemen's club, staffed by men of independent means. Harold's position was prestigious, and would soon become salaried.

The two tripmates carried on a correspondence. Mary-Russell wanted their relationship to be platonic, while Harold was intent on wooing her. She initially rebuffed his advances, stating in a letter written October 2, 1910:

> [W]hen you spoke to me I gave you some hope, which was wrong, I told you that you might ask me again sometime; forgive me, I did not realize what I said, and, in order now to save us both pain in the future, I tell you finally that it could never be.
>
> But there has never been a time when one does not need a good friend, and of all times it is now that I need one most.

So, when you are 'skooting' through Germantown in your auto, stop at 121, and I will know that I have gained a friend.

Harold made it a point to "skoot" by frequently in the big car they called the Blue Choo Choo, and persistence won the day. Soon, he was pursuing an earnest courtship. True to his training, Harold applied scientific methods to his romance. In a little pocket calendar, he kept a meticulous record of his dates with Mary-Russell, showing the time as well as the type of occasion according to the following codes: T=theater, A=auto, C=call, D=dinner, H=home, O=opera.

Harold and Mary-Russell saw each other at least once a week beginning in October 1910. As the courtship continued, Mary-Russell warmed up to Harold. By the end of the year, they were seeing each other nearly every day.

In 1911, the courtship intensified, and it was clear to Mary-Russell that Harold wanted to marry her. On March 15, she went to Provincetown to visit two of her mates from the 1909 Selkirk expedition, Bub and Rosie, who had fallen in love with each other on the trip and were married not long thereafter. Perhaps seeing the fruits of this successful Selkirk romance convinced Mary-Russell that such things were possible, or perhaps Harold simply won her over. In any event, not long after this visit, she agreed to marry him. In his pocket calendar he noted: "Engaged May 13, 1911. Full moon on North Valley Hill. Whippoorwills whippering."

HAROLD S. COLTON,
AGE 20, 1901

Immediately after her engagement, Mary-Russell paid her last visit to her "childhood paradise," Broadwater Island. Tremendously touched by her stay, she tried to recapture all the feelings of her youth, bidding farewell to her childhood and life as a single woman. She saw her haunts of old in a new light as she meditated upon the past and future. As she wrote Harold,

WEDDING DAY
IN PHILADELPHIA, 1912

Ever since I can remember, I have wanted to know, but now that I have known you, I believe I am the most curious person alive, for you have taught me a thousand little ways of getting pleasure, which before, have passed unnoticed or trodden underfoot. And as my sense of appreciation and enjoyment become more keen, I realize what a wonderfully well ordered world we live in, how everything is planned even the most insignificant, and I am happy to be a part of the one great life. And always my faith is growing stronger and my peace more lasting.

After the engagement, Mary-Russell and Harold visited relatives and friends, giving everyone the news and making introductions. Letters of congratulation received by the groom from his family and friends indicated that the family liked Mary-Russell upon meeting her and thought that Harold had chosen well. Mary-Russell's family circle likewise approved of the marriage.

The Presser home in Germantown, Pennsylvania, was the site of the May 23, 1912, wedding. Both Mary-Russell and Harold disliked ostentation, and invited only twelve guests, all of them family, friends, or servants. The reception, a garden party, was held in the Presser's large backyard. Soon after, the newlyweds left on their honeymoon, taking the train and stopping first in Chicago, where they spent several days before going on to the Valley Ranch near Pecos, New Mexico. After their arrival in Pecos on May 30, Mary-Russell wrote to her mother:

It's great out here, and being married is all right, much finer than I anticipated, even, though of course, it all depends on the man, and I certainly have the right one, and as he seems to think the same of me, we get along real well, considering we've been married almost two weeks.

We ride and hike over the mesas and along the roaring Pecos, and paint and read and sleep and eat and are both perfectly fine. I have 6 sketches already, it is a great country to paint in, and the kit works finely.

This morning we are walking down to Pecos village for me to sketch and soon I am going to ship you a bunch of sketches. . . .

Your baby

After a week at Valley Ranch, they went to Taos and Santa Fe. From Santa Fe they took a train to Albuquerque, Harold reporting that "On the train Fairy tried to paint some of the mountain ranges that we passed but it was too wiggly."

Ben Jacobs, the man who had convinced Harold to participate in the 1910 Selkirk trip, and his wife Kate, also newlyweds, joined the Coltons at the Alvarado Hotel in Albuquerque on June 9. Mary-Russell wrote:

Ben and Kate were here when we arrived, and we are having lots of fun to-gether. . . . [We plan to stay around Laguna-Acoma a day or two] . . . and then move on to Flagstaff, Arizona, probably by freight train, in order not to miss any of the wonderful desert country, for all passenger trains pass through at night.

We are both just as well and happy as we can be and so are Ben & Kate, and you wouldn't know your little girl, for she can pass for a Mexican with ease. Harold watches over me with tender care, and won't let me do half the things I wish to. I know you would be surprised to see how able he is to take care of me, he won't even let me eat recklessly.

I'm doing my best to take care of him too, for I never can do enough for him, and he likes being taken care of too. And so we are as ideally happy as the children of a dream, and the best of it is, I know we shall never wake up.

Boarding the train on June 10, the foursome traveled west to Laguna, New Mexico, where they got off an hour before midnight and camped nearby. The following day, they hired a wagon and driver, who took them eighteen miles to Acoma. Camping overnight at the base of Enchanted Mesa, they explored the village the next day and returned to Laguna, where they climbed back on the train at 11 P.M. By morning, they had reached Adamana, Arizona, and from there they explored the Petrified Forest.

When they were ready to reboard the train, they found some resistance from the conductor. Harold described it in a letter to his mother:

> Late in the afternoon the California Limited came along and we in our old camp clothes, looking like such bums that when we got on the conductor told us it was an extra fare train, and when he found that we were willing to pay 60¢ extra to go to Flagstaff, seemed surprised. Fairy and I went in the diner and were taken for a bit of local color. People asked us about the country thru which we were passing and we had answers for them.

A few hours later, the party disembarked at Flagstaff on June 13, again at 11 at night. The conductor recognized them as honeymooners and called out the stop as "Niagara Falls." Though the Coltons had been in Flagstaff briefly in 1910, after their stay at the Grand Canyon, they had not spent any time there. This time they stayed in the town that was to figure prominently in their future.

Harold and Mary-Russell elected to take a room in a hotel, while Ben and Kate headed into the woods to camp. The next day, the Coltons hired a team of horses and a wagon and joined Ben and Kate, who had set up a beautiful camp on Elden Mesa. As they visited, they made plans for the activities of the following day.

Mary-Russell wrote what happened next:

> The next day we beat it for the great volcanic San Francisco Peaks, map in hand & packs on backs. That night we reached a tank or fine water hole at an altitude of 8000 & some feet in a beautiful forest of yellow pine. The next day we carried our packs up to nearly eleven thousand feet (Flagstaff is 7000 ft.) & camped by a snow bank which we melted for cooking, kept the fire up all night. We started at four, in the dark without packs for the peaks, it was Sunday the 16th. The sun rose as we reached the snow crest, the ground was frozen hard & we looked down from the divide & earliest spring into the great crater of the ancient volcano, now covered with down timber, and very drear and strange. We climbed the knife edge & reached the first peak, Mt. Fremont at seven &

*gazed across the Painted Desert to the Grand Canyon and all about the foot of
the peaks lay a sea of little volcanoes long ago asleep, some held lakes in their
throats, & everywhere the shimmering desert and grim lava. I waited on this
peak 12 thousand 2 hundred & fifty high & while H. climbed Mt. Agassiz looked
on this strange world. (Agassiz 3 hundred ft. higher). The altitude has no effect
whatever on either of us. That evening we came half way down to Flagg and
camped at an ideal little spring in the pines. The next evening we tramped into
Flagg at 9:30 o'clock, dogs & horses shied at us.*

Both Mary-Russell and Harold were enthusiastic about the San Francisco
Peaks. As Harold wrote to his mother, "No camp that we have had even in the
Selkirks seems as beautiful." Next on their agenda was a day-trip to the cliff
dwellings at Walnut Canyon; they got there via a hired horse and wagon.

Their sojourn in the little mountain town was a success. Of Flagstaff,
Harold wrote, "What a nice place it would be to make a home."

IN THE COMPANY of Ben and Kate, the Coltons left Flagstaff, taking the
train to the Grand Canyon; they stayed there five days. Mary-Russell sketched
and wrote letters, while Harold and Ben hiked to the Colorado River and
back. It was during this Grand Canyon sojourn that Mary-Russell and Harold
discovered Hopi arts and crafts. Harold wrote, "We bought two old Hopi
blankets—rash ones we are—and a basket—and a Curtis photograph. There
is another rug we want so we have to give the Hopi House a wide berth."

After the Grand Canyon visit, the honeymooners boarded the train and
continued west. They stopped at Los Angeles, from which they went into the
Sierras, camping at El Portal, the western gateway to Yosemite. They spent
more than two weeks camping and hiking in the Sierras, then traveled north to
Mount Shasta, then Portland, Seattle, Vancouver, and Victoria. From Victoria,
the Coltons—finally by themselves—went into the Selkirks. Mary-Russell
wrote her mother:

*We will take it easy, for I am to have plenty of time to paint & lounge around in
the beautiful flowery meadows patched with snow & running with crystal brooks.
May I never grow too old to drag myself to these worlds of eternal life & peace.*

They explored the Canadian Rockies, Banff, and Lake Louise before rejoining Ben and Kate at Spokane. Mary-Russell kept her mother informed as to their progress:

We are both in splendid health & intend to continue to exercise & keep in the same. He has gotten fat & Mr. LaForme declares, looks ten years younger, & several times I have been taken for a little girl.

We went on the train not long ago, when we were in camp costume. Two young fellows, bakers by profession working their way through the country, were much interested in us & asked all sorts of questions. Finally one said, "But does the little girl carry a pack too?" Then we were talking of the country & I spoke of being out before, when one said, "My you must have started coming out here when you were awful little." Wasn't that good for an old married lady? . . . So you can see how the summer has effected [sic] us.

Once again heading east, they took the train to Salt Lake City, where they did a bit of sightseeing. Then the Coltons went on alone to Yellowstone, where they spent a week before returning home. Their wonderful summer of exploration was at an end.

DURING THE HONEYMOON, their new home, Singing Wood, a present from Harold's father, was under construction in Ardmore, Pennsylvania. It was not yet ready upon their return, so they stayed with Harold's parents at Bryn Mawr until it was finished. Harold described Singing Wood as a home in the English-cottage style, embowered in dogwood trees in a dense forest of chestnuts and beeches. On two-and-a-half acres of land, it was only about two miles from Longmeadow, the home of Harold's parents, so frequent visits were possible. Harold's sister, Mildred Colton Esty, lived next door.

In the spring of 1913, Singing Wood was ready and the Coltons moved in, settling into married life. They were assisted by a full-time cook, a full-time maid, and a combination gardener and handyman whose services they shared with Harold's sister. Singing Wood was near the Pennsylvania Railroad, and Harold commuted by rail to work. The home included a large art studio, where Mary-Russell painted and did a considerable amount of restoration on paintings owned by the Colton family. (American artist Charles Wilson Peale was Harold's great-great-grandfather and the family owned some of his work.)

Early in 1913, Harold attended a lecture given by Dr. Frederick Munson, who showed color slides of the Navajo and Hopi Indians and the country in which they lived. The presentation so impressed Harold that he was inspired to learn more about these fascinating people, whose art the Coltons had collected on their honeymoon. Through the Museum of the American Indian, he gained an introduction by correspondence to Don Lorenzo Hubbell, a prominent trader located in Ganado, Arizona, in the heart of Indian country. Hubbell agreed to set up a tour of the Indian lands for the Coltons in the summer of 1913.

In June, the Coltons went West again, with Harold's sister Suzanne, eighteen, and the Coltons' first cousin, Coleman Sellers III, twenty. Mary-Russell reported to her mother from the train as it moved through Kansas:

> *All of yesterday it seemed a dream. I could not realize that I was really on my way once more, to the charmed land that I love so well, but today it comes to me strongly that I will soon be there, as free as the vast plains and the vast sky once more to be uplifted to the face of the Lord upon his mighty mountains and to feel again our close kinship with everything animate & inanimate, one with the great eternal life. In short the "wanderlust" is upon me, the same that reached out to my father & to our ancestors beckoning them over the seas & into the unknown. . . .*

The group traveled by train to Glorietta, New Mexico, where they disembarked and spent a few days at Valley Ranch, the place where Harold and Mary-Russell began their honeymoon the year before. The quartet then undertook an ambitious hike over the Sangre de Cristo mountains, taking along two pack burros and a wagon to carry their supplies. From Valley Ranch, they hiked northward up the Pecos River Valley and across the Santa Barbara Pass at the crest of the Sangre de Cristos. Next, they went down to Taos Pueblo, then coursed southward via San Juan Pueblo, Santa Clara Pueblo, and the Puyé Ruins to Santa Fe. After resting a couple of days in Santa Fe, they left the wagon and footed it easterly over the Sangre de Cristos, working their way back to Valley Ranch.

They said good-bye to Valley Ranch and took the train to Gallup, arriving

CAMPING IN THE SANGRE DE CRISTO MOUNTAINS OF NEW MEXICO,
1913. MARY-RUSSELL'S LONG HAIR IS SHOWN.
SHE USUALLY WORE IT UP.

there at four in the morning on July 24. The only place open was the Commercial House, a saloon. The women looked at each other, shrugged, and decided that they had to wash up and change clothes, so they went in and used the restroom (this was the only time in her life that Mary-Russell entered an establishment that served hard liquor). After refreshing themselves, they breakfasted at the Harvey House and took a look around the town, which Mary-Russell described as, "An uncompromising row of bald faced stores & saloons. Thick smoke from the mines smutched the sunrise. The streets were full of mud holes & poor sanitation & there was not a green thing in sight."

J. C. Cotton of Gallup was a partner of Hubbell, and at Cotton's store they were to pick up saddle horses, a wagon, and two guides, all arranged for by Hubbell. The guides appeared, but one was drunk and had to be replaced. Finally, they mounted up and rode toward Zuni Pueblo, camping en route. Mary-Russell wrote her mother:

We pitched camp against a sandstone mesa on a sage flat & were getting supper when an Indian family drove up & pitched camp nearby. They were Zunis on

their way home, two men, a young squaw & several children in a covered wagon
with several loose horses & colts. They visited us after supper & we held a con-
versation liberally interspersed with candy & much laughter as neither could
speak the language of the other.

The heavens were wonderful, crowded with stars & the moon made the night
as light as day. Not far away our men moved back & forth across the fire & the
white wagon cover loomed palely in the night, while a little way off a roaring
juniper fire glowed red on the Indians' covered wagon & their squatting fig-
ures grouped about the blaze while the horses loomed darkly in the pale light
& we fell asleep listening to the gentle tink-a-tonk, tink-a-tonk of the horse
bells nearby.

The next day they reached Zuni and set up a camp, staying five days.
Although everyone in the party became ill from drinking contaminated water,
they mustered the strength to do a bit of sightseeing until their health
returned. As part of this sightseeing, they were able to watch a kachina dance
at the pueblo. On July 28, Mary-Russell went into the pueblo and had a nice
experience, which she described to her mother: "I sketched in the dance court,
attracting attention from old & young. Everyone smiles upon us, there was
much laughter everywhere. I did not hear a cross word in Zuni."

The next day, they visited Toyallan Mesa, which they climbed, camping
nearby at night. Mary-Russell reported to her mother that in Zuni she had had
an "orgy of painting."

Finally, on July 31, they rode back to Gallup, where they set up camp outside town. Harold's cousin Cora Burnham and her husband Lewis joined
them, arriving on the train in early August. Mary-Russell wrote to her mother,
"Cora & Lewis are with us & we are having more fun than ever, these desert
camps are so fine, never sleep under a tent but all six in a row under the vast
spangled sky."

Once the group broke camp at Gallup, they went by horse and buggy to
Ganado, the site of Hubbell's main trading post. The trip took two days.

The morning following their arrival, they left for Canyon de Chelly,
reaching Chinle on August 7. They rode down into the canyon and camped by
the side of a stream at the base of thousand-foot high cliffs, the walls of which

were studded with ancient dwellings. On August 8 and 9, they explored the area, going into Canyon del Muerto with a guide. On August 10, they headed back to Ganado, where they camped near the trading post for several days. During this stay they became friends of Hubbell, who dropped in every morning for breakfast and taught them about Indian arts, crafts, and customs. Mary-Russell wrote of Hubbell:

> *Mr. Hubbell is Ganado, in fact he is the man in all this big country. He is an elderly man, most cultivated, whose mother was a Mexican. He was born & raised in this country.*
>
> *The Indians in fact everyone adore him & come for hundreds of miles to trade with him at the long low adobe store on the baked brown plain.*

While there, they witnessed a large gathering of Navajos, who had come to Ganado for Hubbell-sponsored games. Harold wrote:

> *In order to keep in touch with the Indians he has every once and a while a chicken pull and horse races which brings to Ganado—his capital—Indians from far and near. . . . You can ride days in the Navajo country and hardly see a soul. Offer a prize for a horse race and they spring out of the ground by hundreds all dressed in velvet shirts and bedecked in silver ornaments, a riot of color and action.*

Mary-Russell enjoyed the games, writing to her mother, "It's great fun, everybody rushes in on horseback as best he can, & sometimes you find yourself packed in by Navajos as far as the eye can reach, great shaggy headed wild fellows, but all kind & friendly. They like me, & let me push in to the front row, talking Navajo & smiling the while."

From Ganado they rode horses to Keams Canyon, the site of another Hubbell trading post, then to Polacca on the Hopi reservation, encountering Hopis for the first time in their lives. Tom Pavatea ran a trading post for his Hopi brethren there, and rented a little stone house to the Colton party.

Using Polacca as a base, they visited the Hopi villages and saw a Snake Dance at Walpi. Ex-president Theodore Roosevelt was also a spectator at the dance, in the company of Hubbell and Arizona's Governor Hunt.

Mary-Russell collected Hopi crafts on this visit, supplementing those purchased during their honeymoon. The party returned to Gallup, and took the train to the Grand Canyon. Harold wrote, "The Canyon is as wonderful as ever and Fairy is getting many sketches."

Following the Grand Canyon visit, the party broke up. Suzanne Colton and Coleman Sellers went home. Cora and Lewis Burnham went to Redlands, California. Harold and Mary-Russell went to Santa Barbara, where Mary-Russell wrote her mother from the Potter Hotel:

> *It's an awful chore getting dressed & washed of mornings now, after going for a month with only 3 baths & taking one's clothes off 3 times, life seems terribly complicated.*
>
> *Riding for a month caused me to lose flesh, & when I return you will be surprised to find that you have a hipless daughter. It takes eight pins to hold me together now & I feel myself rapidly coming to "galluses" for my skirts hang in great pleats about me & I am a most dilapidated looking person all together. But don't think that I am fading away from ill health for I am solid muscle from head to heel & have been enjoying good health all summer. I can be in the saddle from dawn to dark, ride forty-five miles a day, without feeling tired, so you see dear, I am not an ill woman, in spite of hipless condition.*

After a night in Santa Barbara and a night in Monterey, the Coltons took the train to Portland, where they stayed for a few days then boarded the Great Northern railroad, rejoining the Burnhams at Belton, Montana, on September 8.

The two couples spent seven days at the newly created Glacier National Park, then packed up their camp clothes and climbed aboard the train for home, reaching Philadelphia in mid-September.

SOON AFTER HER return, Mary-Russell put on a public display of her Hopi artifacts in Philadelphia. It was well received and encouraged her interest in Hopi arts and crafts.

On the heels of this show, Mary-Russell and some of her fellow graduates of the Philadelphia School of Design for Women held a large and well-attended exhibition in Philadelphia, all of them contributing works. Mary-

Russell exhibited twenty-five paintings, sixteen of which were scenes of the Southwest.

Early in 1914, Mary-Russell learned that she was pregnant. The extended family followed the progress of Mary-Russell's pregnancy through the summer, and, as the end of her term drew near, anxiously awaited the outcome. The Coltons' first child, Joseph Ferrell Colton, was born at Singing Wood on August 30, 1914. When Harold's family heard the news, they were ecstatic. Harold's sister Suzanne described the scene for them in a letter:

We all nearly threw one grand and glorious fit—the whole family in one grand burst of affection fell into one another's arms—kissing and hugging to beat the band. Father going around with a puffed out chest, mother rushing about with one shoe on and one shoe off and with a world wide grin upon her beauteous visage were sights for the sinful and oppressed.

When Harold wrote his parents, he described the delivery:

Poor Fairy had 14 hours of labor and then Dr. McCloud had to call in another doctor, Dr. Bernard, and etherize her and use the forceps. It has left her very weak but Miss Herrstrom says that both mother & son are out of danger now. Dr. McCloud assures us that from now on it will be like any other case. Fairy has recovered from the ether and then fell into a peaceful sleep from which she wakened without any discomforts.

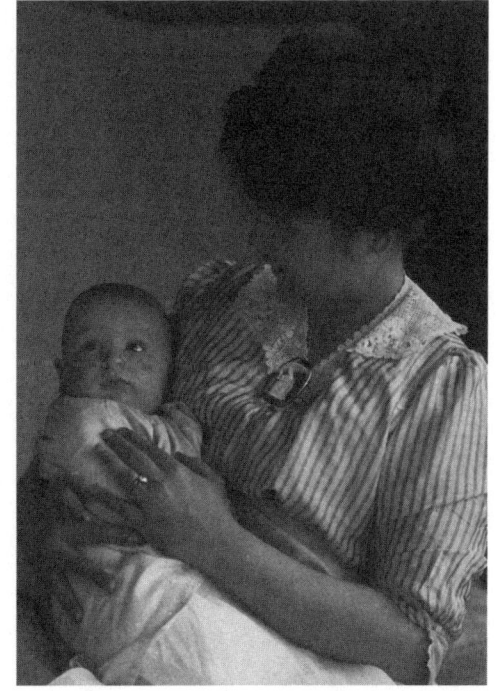

MARY-RUSSELL AND JOSEPH FERRELL COLTON, 1914

The baby was duly visited and admired by all the relatives. Soon, life at Singing Wood adjusted to a family of three Coltons.

IN 1915, THE little family spent its summer vacation at the home of the senior Coltons, Faraway, at Greenings Island, Maine. Getting there was no easy feat, as Harold later described it:

> We drove the Cadillac to Mt. Desert. Ferrell was 9 months old. Traveling with a baby required more logistics than our camping trips in the Southwest or in British Columbia. We had to arrange to get a special brand of milk, called certified milk, at proper intervals. We stopped about 4 every afternoon, a rule my friend, Dr. George Kemmerer, an experienced camper recommended, "Always stop at the first good camping place after four." These camping places were, in our case small New England Inns. After getting settled, I had to make up Ferrell's formula, while the nurse and Mary-Russell washed the diapers. We carried some rope and we draped the wet diapers all over our bedroom. By 9 p.m. we were through our chores and ready for bed.

Although Harold and Mary-Russell were to continue to spend some summers in Maine, they had by this time fallen in love with the West and would avail themselves of every opportunity to go there.

Chapter Three

Travels in the West

IN 1916 THE Coltons decided to go West again. As Harold noted:

Ferrell was only twenty months old; so we could not jaunt around the Southwest as we had done in 1913. Of all the places we had previously visited, Flagstaff, Arizona, seemed to offer the best possibilities, particularly if we could find a place to locate outside the town.

Harold corresponded with V. M. Slipher, an astronomer at Flagstaff's Lowell Observatory whom he had met at a scientific conference. He asked Slipher to recommend a place in Flagstaff where they could stay, and Slipher put him in touch with longtime resident Mrs. C. A. (Ella) Greenlaw, whose family owned a ranch two miles east of town. Ella's husband Charles and his brother Edward operated the Greenlaw Lumber Mill nearby.

Mrs. Greenlaw agreed to build a two-room shack for the Coltons if they would rent it for the summer, and to provide meals at the ranch house. The Coltons arrived early in June with a governess for Ferrell, Ethel Rishworth, whom they called "Richie." Harold and Mary-Russell slept in one of the two rooms, and Ferrell slept in the other. Richie slept in a "Gloucester hammock out under the trees."

East Coast friends joined the Colton family as well. Isabel Branson

Cartwright, one of Mary-Russell's art-school classmates and dear friend, came to Flagstaff with her husband and camped north of town most of the summer on a pasture owned by C. J. Babbitt. The couples enjoyed touring the area together.

One day, they noticed a number of cowboys and Indians coming into town. Richie asked what the occasion was and was told that the crowds were coming in for the "broncho-busting." To the delight of the locals, Richie provided a little Eastern Dude humor when she asked what happened when the "bronchos" burst.

IN MID-JULY, leaving Ferrell in Richie's care, Harold and Mary-Russell took a nine-day trip using horses supplied by the Greenlaws; as was their habit, they were curious about the area and wanted to explore it. They descended into Oak Creek Canyon and camped at West Fork, then went to Sedona, where they "camped in broiling sun on the side of a red hill over a ranch where we procured alfalfa for the horses." The next day, they headed south to Beaver Creek via Bell Rock. Traveling through what is now the densely settled area of the Village of Oak Creek, they reported that they saw not a single house or soul the entire day. The road they followed was two wagon tracks etched into the red dirt.

By the end of the day, they reached the Billy Back Ranch at Montezuma's Well, where they accepted Mr. and Mrs. Back's invitation to camp. After visiting Montezuma's Castle the next day, they returned home on the new Blue Grade Road, which at that time was complete only as far as Rattlesnake Tanks. After an overnight stay at Stoneman Lake, they returned to Flagstaff via Mormon Lake.

Once back at Greenlaw's, they made it a routine to ride every day, exploring and looking for inspiring scenes for Mary-Russell to paint. On a picnic one day, little Ferrell picked up an object and held it out to his father, who inspected it and declared it to be a potsherd. Harold then scrutinized the spot on which they were sitting and discovered that it was littered with artifacts of various types. Intrigued, he and Mary-Russell spent the next several outings in search of other sites.

They were so taken with their discoveries that they went to Los Angeles and its Museum of the Southwest to learn more about Arizona's prehistory. There, they met with Dr. Munk, who had a library of eight thousand books about Arizona, larger than any collection in the state itself. With his help, they checked all available sources and found that no one had made any effort to catalog, preserve, or protect ancient sites around Flagstaff except at Walnut Canyon, which had been designated as a National Monument in 1915. Otherwise, the sites were either unknown or—if known—pot-hunted and otherwise vandalized.

Although archaeologists had discovered the Southwest and some exciting finds had been made on the Colorado Plateau, little work had been done in the Flagstaff region.

After spending several days on the coast, the Coltons returned to Flagstaff, determined to do what they could to find, record, map, and protect ruin sites. Their private, systematic study, a work that lasted for years, was the first archaeological survey of the Flagstaff area.

THE COUPLE HAD experienced some of the Southwest's Indian cultures during earlier trips, and now, stimulated by their discovery of ruins and their research at the museum, were eager to learn more. Soon after their return from Los Angeles, Harold and Mary-Russell rented a couple of mules and a wagon and set out for the Hopi mesas to see the Snake Dances at Hotevilla and Oraibi. They also wanted to see Tuba City, a place they had only recently heard about. On the way they kept their eyes open for possible ruins. It turned out to be one of the most adventurous trips they ever took.

After a day's travel north along what is today Highway 89, they came within sight of the Painted Desert, a place that became their favorite. As always when she went into the field, Mary-Russell carried her sketch book; in the colorful Painted Desert country, she constantly found scenes that delighted her eye and sparked her artistic imagination.

Crossing the Little Colorado River at Cameron, they camped in Moenkopi Wash and then pushed on. After two more days of riding, they reached Tuba City, where they were welcomed by S. S. Preston, a veteran

Indian trader, who invited them to dinner. Harold described the appearance of Tuba City at the time as

> *rows of Poplars and buildings of red sandstone and adobe. Soon we were driving up the main street of the town. . . Tuba City is in a real oasis. It is made possible by a gushing spring of pure water that pours out among the sand hills on the top of the mesa. The main street is half a mile long.*

Unhitching the mules from the wagon, they saddled them and rode to Castle Rock and Moenkopi, where they turned back to Tuba City for a two-day rest. Then, restored, they hitched up the mules again, forded Moenkopi Wash, and began the long uphill climb along a primitive sandy road to the top of Howell Mesa. They were laboring mightily, having much trouble with the balky mules, when a Hopi named Poli, riding a pony, joined them. He offered to drive the mules to the top, and was able to coax them to within a hundred feet of the crest, a point beyond which they refused to budge. Poli helped the Coltons carry all their supplies from the wagon to the top of the mesa. The mules were then convinced to take the lightened wagon to the top.

As it was dusk by then, Harold and Mary-Russell went about a mile farther and set up a camp, which Poli shared with them. During the night, the mules strayed, but Poli recaptured them in the morning and they continued on to the foot of Third Mesa, where they set up another camp. Poli told them that he would ride his pony home to Hotevilla on the mesa top, spend the night there, and return the next morning to guide them into the village. True to his word, he showed up the following morning, and as Harold related, "Mary-Russell walked with him while I drove. He told her the legends of his people. Showed her the different plants and told their uses to his people. We had a most interesting time."

Outside Hotevilla, they stopped for lunch; as Harold recalled, it was "beside a milky tank full of semi-transparent tadpoles. Filling our water bags, we gathered up a number of the tadpoles by accident, and we had to use care when we wanted a drink."

They left Poli at Hotevilla, and went down to the Hubbell Trading Post at Lower Oraibi, where they saw the last Snake Dance ever performed there. Dr. Byron Cummings, dean of Southwest archaeology, was also visiting Oraibi, and the Coltons introduced themselves. Following that, they saw another Snake Dance at Hotevilla and then started home to Flagstaff.

The Coltons' return trip was also full of adventures, one of which required Mary-Russell to wade across the Little Colorado River in a raging flood. But as Harold wrote his mother,

We returned in fine physical shape as "strong as lions." I had a fifteen day beard as Mary-Russell had forgotten my razor in the hurry of getting off. She had discarded her skirt and taken to bloomers quite unblushingly, and on the whole trip wore her hair in pigtails.

Upon their return to Flagstaff, they canceled their boarding arrangement with the Greenlaws, and Mary-Russell began cooking their own meals, which was a big improvement, as neither thought much of Mrs. Greenlaw's cuisine.

NEAR THE END of the summer of 1916, the Coltons learned from newspapers that there was an outbreak of infantile paralysis, polio, on the East Coast. This report gave them deep concern for Ferrell's health, and the couple decided that Harold would return to Philadelphia alone to resume his teaching duties. Mary-Russell and Ferrell would remain in Flagstaff until cool weather in the East ended the epidemic; they would then rejoin Harold.

Mary-Russell found herself alone with Ferrell and Richie in Flagstaff for about five weeks, from near the end of September through the month of October. It was their first separation since marriage. Harold and Mary-Russell missed each other keenly and wrote daily. On September 24, 1916, she wrote to Harold, "All morning I painted under the trees, I have started a big canvas of the Dry Beaver country, tomorrow I will finish it. I feel very much in the painting spirit."

She also continued to roam the area and was constantly on the lookout for Indian ruins and relics, finding many. The ruins moved her. As she wrote to her mother,

I am writing in my favorite spot, a little mound of stones covered with pine needles and blooming things, the sun always shines upon it, the tall pines breathe gently about it, it is very still here always; and some how I feel that

the little old people, whose home this once was were happy here. Perhaps they were young people then, and did not dream how long their happiness should haunt a few gray stones and bits of pottery. These are the only ghosts in which I believe, these eloquent personal things; what man has made with his hands, in his joy or his sorrow, the home in which he has lived, they are forever his, and through the ages, breathe to us who pass, the spirit of their maker.

In a letter to Harold written on October 14, she described another trip:

I collected pottery for you, there is any quantity there, black & white, red & black, pinched & plain, also I found half of a finely chiseled white opalescent stone spear point. It was snowing when I got there & the quaking asps were the most gorgeous vivid gold against the cold gray.

I must now place my feet in the oven before going to bed, I know, it is not done in polite society but that is one of the compensations of shack life in the back woods.

She found much to enjoy in her solitude:

As I walked up the lane in the last golden glow a coyote called from Switzer's Mesa & presently a whole chorus joined in from somewhere up back of Dry Lake Mountain. I stood and listened to the voices of the wild and thrilled beneath those wondrous shining peaks, and presently as I looked, they changed to rose, glowing like dream mountains in the land that never was, then slowly they grew cold and so very very awesome and I hurried home to the warmth of our little shack.

Harold sent her one of her favorite types of reading material, a mystery, and Mary-Russell reported that "The detective story came today and I am going to jump into bed and there read in luxury." In the same letter, she indicated that conditions stimulated her artistically: "Tomorrow I paint. It is upon me again, the fever."

On the next-to-final day of her stay, October 23, 1916, Mary-Russell took one of her solitary rides. Mounted on Pumpkin, one of the Isbell's horses, she

[R]ode up past the Greenlaw mill and struck in directly toward Elden from right near the Winslow, [Grand] canyon sign post. Crossing the lumber railroad I soon

came out upon a very high mound, and suddenly realized that I had found the largest Pueblo, we have yet come upon. I should say it had been quite equal in size to Walpi, the buildings at the northern end having been at least 2 story, & I believe 3 story, the entire mound is over 15 feet high. It faced north & south, it is undoubtedly the terminus of the Pottery trail, & by far the most impressive we have seen. Tomorrow I return to make measurements & a sketch & collect pottery for you. I was quite thrilled over my find.

This ruin, which came to be named Elden Pueblo, is one of the most important in the Flagstaff region and has been the object of study for decades since Mary-Russell, Ferrell, and Richie returned home safely in late October 1916. In early 1917, Mary-Russell felt tired and miserable. In February, she had a bout of tonsillitis; after a few days rest, she recovered, feeling peppy for a while. Soon she was dragging again, so she went back to the doctor, who this time found the cause: she was pregnant.

On April 6, 1917, the United States declared war on Germany and entered World War I. Harold was then thirty-six years old, father of one child and expecting another, and as such was exempt from military service. However, he felt obligated to do his bit, so he volunteered. He was accepted in a Home Guard unit, but wanted to be in the real army. As the summer waxed, Harold soldiered on the weekends. His Home Guard company was called out a few times but its only duties were to transport troops, guard buildings, and perform other tame activities.

On September 4, 1917, Mary-Russell gave birth to the Coltons' second child, a son they named Sabin Woolworth Colton IV, in honor of Harold's father. The Coltons anticipated that the delivery might be difficult, so they made arrangements to have the baby delivered in a hospital rather than at home. It was indeed a difficult delivery and though the baby was healthy, Mary-Russell's own health took a downward turn. This birth seems to have disturbed her equilibrium, and for the rest of her life, she suffered one complaint after another as well as a persistent nervous disorder.

AT THE BEGINNING of 1917, Mary-Russell and some of her friends from the Philadelphia School of Design for Women organized a group they called

"The Ten Philadelphia Women Painters." (They changed the name to "The Ten" after they admitted sculptors and some of the group's members—including Mary-Russell—moved from Philadelphia.) As The Ten, they pledged themselves to hold annual exhibitions to which each member contributed original work. No mere self-flattering collection of dilettantes, the group's members were all serious and gifted artists. Most had studied at the Philadelphia School of Design for Women, though a few were graduates of the Pennsylvania Academy of Fine Arts. As one of their aims, they vowed to "[show] just the work they wished to present, in the most dignified and harmonious manner." The exhibitions of The Ten were held at various locations in Philadelphia, starting in February 1917, and were supplemented by traveling exhibitions that they sent to various halls within and outside of Pennsylvania.

IN 1918, HAROLD was finally accepted into the regular army. That July, he went to work in Washington, D. C., without pay and without a commission, preparing geographical handbooks in a Military Intelligence unit. His family remained behind at Singing Wood. With her husband absent, everyday chores, particularly taking care of the children, taxed Mary-Russell greatly. She told Harold that she could not keep a big house by herself, as it was too much for her, even with the help of the few remaining servants who had not been drained away by military service or defense work. And, although she was game, she was so overwhelmed by the tasks of housekeeping and child-raising that she could not find time to paint.

Then illness struck. Sabin's health was poor during the summer, with a complaint that Mary-Russell called "milk sickness," and Ferrell had a cold. Mary-Russell watched with horror as Ferrell's cold worsened and turned into life-threatening pneumonia. Then she herself fell desperately ill with influenza, and was in critical condition for nine days, a victim of the Great Flu Epidemic that was then sweeping the world and killing millions. She wrote to Harold that she might have died but for the fact that her mother was there to nurse her. Eventually, all three patients recovered.

MARY-RUSSELL IN THE COLTON APARTMENT IN CHEVY CHASE,
MARYLAND, DURING HAROLD'S WARTIME SERVICE, 1918.
BABY SABIN IS ON LEFT, FERRELL IS ON RIGHT.

HAROLD HAD BEEN promised a captain's commission when he entered active service, but something always came along to block or delay it. The procrastination bothered him, not only because his status without a commission was unclear, but because he did not want to move the family to Washington until the commission had been received. As the summer wore on, Mary-Russell was so unhappy that the Coltons decided she would move to Washington, commission or no commission. Harold found an apartment for the family in Chevy Chase, Maryland, no easy task in the wartime capital area, and the family joined him. Soon after, Harold received his long-promised commission. Harold wrote to his parents:

> *Life down here is pretty rough on Mary Russell. We can get no help of any kind. The congestion in Washington still persists but there are indications that after the first of the year things will ease up a little. If she could only get some one in to do the cleaning, wash the dishes and do the washing for the baby, things would be better.*

In spite of her own difficulties, Mary-Russell found it in herself to reach out to neighbors. As Harold wrote:

> *Mrs. Taylor the wife of the young Lieut. on the third floor was taken ill last week. Mary Russell has had the additional care of Gilbert aged three. Mary Russ has also undertaken to feed the Taylor family and nurse the sick wife as well as to put the apartment in order.*

Wartime upsets notwithstanding, Harold and Mary-Russell found time to publish their first article on archaeology, "The Little-known Small House Ruins in the Coconino Forest," which appeared in the October-December 1918 issue of *Memoirs of the American Anthropological Association*. Their Southwestern summers lived on in their thoughts.

Though the war ended on November 11, 1918, Harold was not discharged until April 1919, following which the family returned to Singing Wood. Promoted to assistant professor at the university, Harold's life resumed its pre-war routine, as did those of his wife and children.

BY THE SUMMER of 1919, the Coltons were able to return to Flagstaff. In part, their purpose was to continue the archaeological survey of Indian ruins that they had begun in 1916. They also intended to excavate one of the sites they had located earlier, in a place they called Picture Canyon, for which they had obtained a federal permit under the aegis of the University of Pennsylvania. Their party consisted of Harold and Mary-Russell, their two sons, and their nurse, Ethel Rishworth. Later they were joined by Cora and Lewis Burnham, the Burnham children (Alan, 6, and Joan, 4) and their nurse.

Upon their arrival in Flagstaff, the Coltons rented rooms at the Weatherford Hotel while they looked for a place to stay. They did not want to return to the Greenlaw Ranch because of the dust kicked up by automobiles driving by on the National Old Trails Highway (later to be named Highway 66) and the bothersome noise of the nearby railroad. Although they had not arranged anything in advance, they were confident that they could find something suitable. One of the places they wanted to inspect was the thirty-eight-acre C. J. Babbitt pasture, the site that had been occupied by Mary-Russell's friend Isabel Branson Cartwright in 1916. After much looking, they concluded that the Babbitt pasture was the most attractive prospect, and rented it for the summer. Their living conditions were improved by a water tap obtained from the city, and they had a carpenter build five tent floors and side walls, which they finished with canvas roofs. They also bought a 1914 Model T pickup which they called *Begay* (Navajo, "son of"), several horses, and a couple of donkeys. They called their camp *Adini Kinlani,* meaning "Thunder City" in Navajo.

Mary-Russell described their location in a letter to her mother: "Our pasture is surely heavenly. We always have a strong breeze & no dust. It is so lovely, all the wild roses are in bloom and there are acres of iris, it is a flower garden."

Once again, they amused themselves by exploring the countryside and hunting for ruins. After the Burnhams joined them, the two couples made three major trips. One was to Wupatki, the first trip to the ancient ruins for both the Coltons and the Burnhams. Getting there required a difficult horseback trek, following loose instructions given by an old-timer, who said that Wupatki was "just around the mesa." Once underway, they encountered a number of mesas, none of which proved to be the gateway to the ruins. Late in the day, as they were about to give up hope, they rounded Woodhouse Mesa and sighted their target.

The second trip was an ambitious multi-day horseback ride in late July. The route echoed the Coltons' 1916 trip, going to Sedona through Oak Creek Canyon. From Sedona, they went to a new camping place between Bell Rock and Court House Rock, where they had an unexpected pleasure, of which Mary-Russell wrote her mother:

As the rains have been terrific, we found pools of water every where in the clean solid rock. Climbing a hundred feet or so, we came upon two perfect bathtubs, the water clear & cool. After riding at a temperature of over a hundred, you can not imagine how alluring this appeared. Cora & I promptly plunged in, like two nymphs high upon the swelling red sandstone, upon the smooth surface of which we afterward did a wild dance of joy.

MARY-RUSSELL, HAROLD, AND FRIENDS ON A MULTI-DAY HORSE RIDE,
PAUSING NEAR BELL ROCK, SOUTH OF SEDONA, ARIZONA, 1919

The next morning they enjoyed the natural pools again:

Started off in fine spirits after morning dip in our elevated bathtub, where I gave a small frog the scare of his life! Knight [a stray dog that had adopted them] followed us up & protested against the impropriety of the proceedings, by reverting to his ancestral coyote howl, previous master probably not in the habit of performing so strangely.

From this idyllic setting they went south along Dry Beaver Creek (which was flowing at the time) and at noon, visited the old stage station below Beaverhead. They then continued south to visit Montezuma's Well, where they stayed with the Billy Back family, who remembered Mary-Russell and Harold from their 1916 visit. After their sojourn here, they went to Camp Verde, of which Mary-Russell wrote, "Of all the desperate awful towns, this is the worst!" Their route next took them to Clear Creek and then to the top of the Mogollon Rim via the terrible old General Crook Road. Finishing at the Tonto Natural Bridge, they camped for a few days before returning home via the Tunnel Road, General Springs, Stoneman Lake, and Mormon Lake.

The third expedition took the couples to Grand Canyon and Havasu Canyon, where they hiked down to the Havasupai village. On this outing, they drove Begay.

During the busy summer, Harold and Mary-Russell found time to work on the excavation of Picture Canyon. They dug enthusiastically, but in an unlearned and clumsy manner that made them blush later, after they had developed some expertise. It was also during this summer sojourn that the Coltons met the Pollocks of Flagstaff, Tom and Mary, who became fast friends.

Before the birth of Sabin, Mary-Russell had handled such activities easily, but was complaining of exhaustion and the need of a rest by the end of the summer. Harold wrote to his mother:

> *Our plans for the future are very uncertain. I have to be home about the 20th of the month [September]. I had hoped to be able to locate Mary-Russell out here somewhere with her horse in a place where she could rest, paint and not have to cook. This seems impossible. There is no place at Flagstaff. The Grand Canyon does not appeal to her. Valley Ranch New Mexico sets too poor a table. The Natural Bridge at Pine is too inaccessible. So I am going to bring her home with me.*

On September 16, 1919, the Coltons broke camp in Flagstaff, leaving the wooden floors and sidewalls of Adini Kinlani behind them, thinking they might be useful in the future. Harold sold Begay to Louise Greenlaw, Ella Greenlaw's daughter. By this time, the Coltons knew that they wanted to return to Flagstaff as often as possible, so they made an arrangement with pioneer merchant W. H. Switzer to store their camping equipment, saddles, and other gear in the loft of his downtown hardware store.

IN 1920, THEY spent the summer at Faraway in Maine, guests of Harold's parents. Realizing that to drive there by automobile, with the children and their nurse and all of their things for a stay of several weeks, would be a major undertaking, Harold came up with what seemed to be a neat solution to the problem. He bought one of the first camp trailers ever manufactured. However, the roads were rough and the trailer kept working itself loose from the hitch, causing an endless string of accidents. On the way back, traveling through New Hampshire, the trailer came loose again. It was the last straw. Harold sold the trailer on the spot and had no use for trailers after that.

The Coltons returned to Flagstaff in the summer of 1921, eager to continue their survey of Indian ruins. Frank Baxter, Harold's friend and an assistant in zoology at the University of Pennsylvania, came with them, as did the children's new nurse, Isabel Brodie. In Flagstaff they bought a 1919 Model T Ford truck. This was an ordinary pickup, but Harold modified it by cutting down the back and adding metal hoops across the bed, which they covered with canvas tenting material. The result was a vehicle they called "El Fordo."

They rented a place north of town, the 1919 site of the Evans Boys' School. On the property were a "real house" and several tents with wooden floors and sides; one tent served as Mary-Russell's studio. There was also a corral and barn. Mary-Russell described the place to her mother:

> *Harold and I are both writing home letters in our tent. We look out to the blue bulk of Elden Mt. and little Henry Ford waiting patiently before the kitchen door. It is very quiet, only the crickets chirping and the far off tinkle of a sheep bell from the lonely camp of the old Spanish herder up on the mesa.*
>
> *In the last two days we have acquired a cook, two horses and a dog. The dog is a near collie. He has simply taken us over, adopted us. The cook is a perfect lady and came today.*
>
> *We have never before been so comfortably fixed out here in fact we are*

enjoying luxury. Our hardest work consists in getting . . . El Fordo started especially when he's cold and morose in the morning, but after he is shoved down hill into the arroyo it always wakes him up and he goes snorting off in fine glee.

The little boys are bursting with health. F's asthma has finally left him entirely. They revel in the nice mud out here and I hardly believe you would recognize your grandsons when time comes for the evening bath and just think we have a shower.

AFTER FINISHING THEIR excavation at Picture Canyon, begun in 1919, one of their chief pleasures that summer was exploring the Painted Desert. They launched a survey of the Wupatki area, a place that was on the edge of the desert and rich in ruins; it was to become one of their favorites.

On August 9, they began a long trip in El Fordo, intending to visit the White Mountains of Arizona and the Chaco ruins of New Mexico. Getting away late due to car trouble, they drove to Meteor Crater and camped at its base. On August 10 they explored the crater, then drove on to Snowflake, camping nearby. The next day they drove through Lakeside, Show Low , and Pinetop, reaching the edge of the Apache Reservation that night, where they camped. The roads were so muddy that instead of continuing into the White Mountains, they veered off to Gallup and stayed at a hotel. From Gallup they planned to go to Chaco and Pueblo Bonito, which was then being excavated by Dr. Neil Judd of the National Geographic Society.

They set out for Chaco on the morning of August 14. Heavy rains made the going difficult, compounded by the fact that there was no real road, just a wagon track. They became stuck in quicksand and had a difficult time extricating the car. As the road got worse and it seemed that the rains would continue, they returned to Gallup. Mary-Russell was so exhausted that they rested for a day there in a hotel, and ultimately gave up on the idea of going to Chaco.

On August 16 and 17 they traveled west, reaching St. Michaels Mission. Here they visited members of the Day family, pioneer trading post operators. The next day, they paid a call to their old friend Don Lorenzo Hubbell, who was, unfortunately, away. Renting horses, the party rode to Chinle, where they saw the ruins at Canyon de Chelly, "as fine as ever."

Keams Canyon and Walpi were next on their agenda. On the 20th they went to Keams Canyon. They had to be helped across the rain-swollen Polacca Wash by Tom Pavatea, the Hopi trader, who used a team of horses to get them to the other side.

Finally, conquering tremendous obstacles, they went to the Snake Dances in the Hopi villages of Mishongnovi and Walpi. They joined a prestigious audience; also watching the dances were newspaper magnate William Randolph Hearst, artist Jimmy Swinnerton, and author D. H. Lawrence. On the way home, they were able to use the new bridge at Leupp, which meant that they no longer had to ford the Little Colorado River at Tolchaco, the site of their mighty struggles with floodwaters and quicksand in 1916.

WHILE EXPLORING WUPATKI in the summer of 1921, the Coltons met Jesse C. Clarke, a Flagstaff postal employee and self-trained archaeologist. Clarke was greatly concerned about the deteriorating condition and pillage of ancient sites around the town, and acted as the unofficial caretaker for Wupatki. When he met the Coltons, he took the opportunity to speak to Mary-Russell and Harold about means of protecting the ruins in the Flagstaff area. After the Coltons returned to Philadelphia, again very pleased with their stay in Flagstaff, Harold carried on a correspondence with Clarke.

EARLY IN 1922, Harold's parents, who had for many years been subjected to Harold and Mary-Russell's glowing accounts of the West, set out to see it for themselves. Harold wrote to them in February:

We were very interested to hear of your glimpse of Flagstaff in the snow. You presented us with a very vivid picture of the scene from the window of your car. I do not want you to feel that I am booming the place but even without its mantle of snow it is without the sordid appearance of the other western towns. The bracing climate gives the inhabitants a great deal of public spirit for a town on the edge of civilization.

While the senior Coltons were on their journey, an important event took place at Singing Wood. As Harold described it to his mother in a letter dated March 11,

We have had today hanging over us for the past month and I am glad that it is over. After Dr. Earnshaw looked Mary Russell over x-rayed her and tested her out and still could find no reason for her nervousness, lack of pep and for her aches and pains, I sent her to Dr. Bernard. He found certain wounds that were caused by the arrival of Sabin in bad shape. They were infected and pouring poison presumably into her blood. He advised having the damaged tissue cut away. For that he advised Dr. Clark.

She was operated on this morning at the University Hospital and is doing well. She is comfortable but weak.

MARY-RUSSELL POSES WITH HER FAVORITE (VERY LARGE) PALETTE, 1922

Mary-Russell also wrote to Harold's parents, making the best of her condition:

> This letter contains a little surprise for you, a pleasant one now.
>
> Yesterday, Dr. John Clark performed a slight operation on me, and removed some rags & tatters from the lower part of my uterus which they believe has been the cause of all my aches & pains.
>
> In the last few years I have carried a heavy burden & now I am hoping that it has rolled from me. . . .
>
> When you dear people return, I shall be as "spry as a cricket."

Although the operation was described to Harold's parents as a minor affair, it was actually a partial hysterectomy, during which Mary-Russell's left ovary was removed. The operation was successful, and Mary was able to travel by summertime, but she never regained her earlier vigor and stamina.

THE SUMMER OF 1922 was spent in Maine, the last of their outings there. At Faraway, Mary-Russell painted many watercolors of marine life and seascapes. They cut short their stay, however; the weather in Maine that summer was foggy and as a result, Ferrell had severe asthma problems. Because of his discomfort, the family left early and went into Canada. They stayed for a few days in Quebec and then headed homeward, driving through a very rural, very French area.

One night they took a room at an inn run by a landlady who spoke little English. Mary-Russell, fussy about cleanliness, had been known to conduct meticulous inspections of hotel rooms; she would even scrub toilet seats. When she turned back the linen on the bed in the French inn, she was horrified, for it was obvious that someone else had slept on the sheets. Bristling with indignation, she insisted that Harold complain to the landlady.

There ensued a heated exchange, with neither Harold nor the French woman understanding more than a few of the words hurled by the other. Soon, however, it was clear that the lady of the house, ablaze with outrage that someone should complain of sheets that had been used by only one previous guest, was demanding that the Coltons leave. Finally, a compromise was reached, the sheets were changed, and the Coltons stayed.

ALTHOUGH THE COLTONS did not go to Flagstaff in 1922, the town continued to have an influence on their lives. From the letters that went back and forth between Harold and J. C. Clarke, it is clear that a seed was planted. Harold later recalled:

> The idea of a museum for Flagstaff grew out of correspondence between
> J. C. Clarke . . . and myself in 1922. We both felt that the scientific resources
> of northern Arizona should be preserved in Arizona as well as in the large
> Eastern museums. The people of Flagstaff had seen members of expeditions
> arriving almost every year at the Santa Fe Railway station and driving away
> into the relatively unknown back country. Later in the season they saw these
> members, now dusty and bearded, return, accompanied by boxes of specimens
> which were shipped away to Eastern centers.

The summer of 1922 also saw unhappy developments in the life of Mary-Russell's mother. Elise's marriage to Theodore Presser was so troubled that she left Presser and came to live with Harold and Mary-Russell, bringing Dysie with her. Once they had moved Elise into their home, Harold and Mary-Russell saw that she was extremely ill. She died at Singing Wood on November 7, 1922, from complications of a bleeding gastric ulcer.

She was buried, not with the Presser family, but in the Houston family plot at the Cave Hill Cemetery in Louisville, beside her first husband Joseph, her daughter Griselda, and her parents. Every Easter thereafter, Mary-Russell sent a bouquet of flowers for their graves. After Elise's death, Harold and Mary-Russell took on the obligation of caring for Dysie. They built a separate apartment for her at Singing Wood and provided for her upkeep until she died in 1925.

The death of her mother was a terrible blow to Mary-Russell, as the two were extremely close. In order to spend more time with her, Harold arranged to take a sabbatical the following semester, the spring term of 1923.

In February 1923, the Coltons—along with the children's nurse, Isabel Brodie—went by train to Tucson, Arizona. They stayed at the Santa Rita Hotel for several days while Harold scoured the area for a suitable place to rent. He found a dilapidated ranch house on the Monthan Ranch, twelve miles east of town near Tanque Verde. Before their arrival, the place had been used

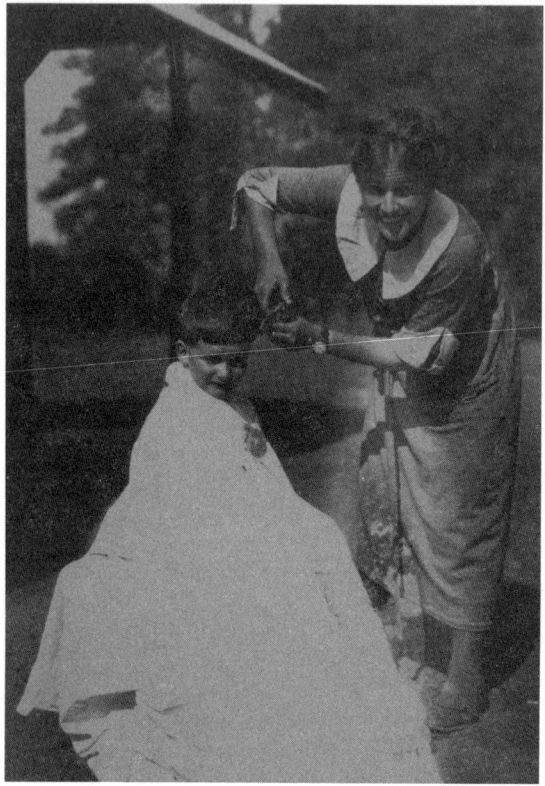

AT THE BABBITT PASTURE CAMP,
FLAGSTAFF; MARY-RUSSELL CUTS
SABIN'S HAIR, 1923.

by moonshiners and as a result, was a mess, with a yard full of spoiled mash and other detritus. After having the place cleaned up, the Coltons hired a cook and a handyman and took up residence.

In March, Harold's sister Suzanne, who had married Robert Thomas Wilson in 1917, came to visit, along with her husband and their son Robert, Jr. They rented horses, and all enjoyed riding around the Tucson area. In addition to the animals, the Coltons got around using a new 1923 Model T Ford sedan with a station wagon body; as was their habit, they named the vehicle: "Petie." It was the first station wagon in Arizona, obtained for them as a result of much effort on the part of Monte Mansfield, a veteran Ford dealer in Tucson. It was such a rarity that people stopped and stared at it.

Because the Arizona roads were so bad, the Coltons had Petie specially fitted out. On the running board were attached three cans: red for gas, gray for water, and blue for oil. Harold installed a special Ruckstell axle, which allowed the vehicle to have four speeds forward and two in reverse. Because Petie's tires were narrow and tended to slice into sand instead of rolling over the top of it, they carried four rolls of chicken wire on the roof, using the wire as a carpet to cross sandy patches. These measures worked, and Petie never failed them.

One day during their stay in Tucson, Harold decided that it was time for Mary-Russell to learn how to drive, and she agreed to try. He seated her at the wheel and they took off down an unpaved country road. She did very well at first, but soon came to a curve. The Model T had as an accelerator a lever that was pushed up or down to control speed, mounted on the steering post. Mary-Russell panicked as she banked into the curve and moved the lever in the wrong direction so that the car sped up and careened around the bend on two wheels. Harold shouted at her to move the lever in the other direction. She promptly did so, brought the car to an immediate halt, stepped out, dusted off her hands and said that was that. She never drove again.

WHEN WARM WEATHER came to the desert in May, the Wilsons returned to Pennsylvania. The Coltons, taking the cook with them, left Tucson and made a leisurely trip northward, sightseeing along the way. They drove over the Black Canyon Highway through Bumble Bee and Cherry Creek Road, finally reaching Sedona, where they stayed for two weeks, waiting for the weather in Flagstaff to warm up. During the wait, they camped on the east bank of Oak Creek, swimming daily in the stream just below the bridge at the foot of the Schnebly Hill Road. There was no store in Sedona at the time and when they wanted groceries they had to drive to Cottonwood, a trip that took three hours each way.

When the weather in the high country improved, they made the final leg of their trip from Sedona to Flagstaff. This was no easy matter—Schnebly Hill's steep grades and Petie's weak engine presented a challenging combination. Harold found a rancher who agreed to take their possessions to the top in his wagon to lighten Petie's load. Even so, it was a struggle. They drove for a short distance until the car overheated, boiling off the water in its radiator. They then blocked the rear wheels with rocks and waited for the engine to cool down, refilled the radiator and drove until it boiled over again, repeating the process all the way to the top. Harold used seven and a half gallons of water getting up Schnebly Hill. They camped at the top that night and then made an easy journey into Flagstaff the following day.

Once again in Flagstaff, they rented the Babbitt pasture as they had in 1919, when they built Adini Kinlani. They set up a new camp, which was located several hundred feet south of the 1919 camp, and did not re-use any part of their old quarters. Happily, they resumed the Flagstaff activities that they had come to love: exploring, ruins hunting, and in general, enjoying the out-door life. They visited the Hopi mesas once more, collecting arts and crafts. It was their aim to host an Indian exhibit at the Arts and Crafts Guild in Philadelphia the following winter, and the visits offered them opportunities to renew contacts.

Their summer stay in Flagstaff was marred only by the fact that Sabin was not his usual active self. Since their stay in Tucson, he had been listless and pale. Ultimately, it was discovered that Sabin's malaise was not the result of a transitory childhood illness, but rather, a much more dangerous condition. While he was in Tucson, the boy had contracted Valley Fever, a disease caused by a fungus that grows in some desert soils; it causes trouble for humans when it becomes airborne and is inhaled. Children born in the desert usually de-velop an immunity, but visitors can become infected. If it becomes established in the lungs, it causes difficulty in breathing, fatigue, fever, and other prob-lems. In some cases it is fatal, leading to a painful, wasting death.

Once back home in Philadelphia, the Coltons consulted all the best doc-tors, but the eastern physicians were unfamiliar with the disease and in spite of everything they could do for him, Sabin died on May 4, 1924. Mary-Russell was distraught. A sensitive person and a highly protective mother, she was devastated by the experience of watching Sabin die and being unable to help him. In retrospect, Harold believed that she never recovered from the ex-perience.

AFTER SABIN'S DEATH, Harold arranged to take part in a project in the state of Washington, hoping that the long trip there and the change of scenery would help take Mary-Russell's mind off Sabin's loss. They drove west through the Great Plains into the Black Hills of South Dakota and saw the Big Horn Mountains, Yellowstone, and Jackson Hole. Mary-Russell wrote to Harold's parents from Yellowstone:

> *I know that you will both be pleased to hear that I have been getting stronger right along; when I first started out I had a right hard struggle, the constant movement helped my mind, but my stomach wouldn't let me eat anything.*
>
> *As soon as we started camping I began to eat a little again, and now*

though I tire pretty easily and sometimes have a bit of a "black spell," you would be surprised how tough I'm getting again. I can eat now too, without being afraid.

Daddy is just too tickled to see me enjoying things again and without a backache! He always worries so when I'm not right.

That is why it has been so long since my last letter, I didn't have the spirit to write.

Now I'm going to lie down for a nice nap, listening to the rain on the roof and the cheerful crackling of the fire.

Mary-Russell was astonished by what she saw at Yellowstone, where travel inside the park was now undertaken by automobile; on her first visit in 1909, it all been done by stagecoach. This significant change within her lifetime made her feel like an old lady, she said.

Eventually, they spent a few days at the University of Washington's marine research laboratory at Friday Harbor on Orcas Island. At the end of the stay, they went south through Salt Lake City, stopping along the route for hiking and sightseeing. Near the end of the summer, they visited the North Rim of the Grand Canyon, then Mesa Verde and Flagstaff, where they spent a few days before heading home.

HAROLD AND HIS Flagstaff friend, amateur archaeologist, J. C. Clarke, made a significant contribution to the preservation of the Indian ruins at Wupatki that year, as described by Harold:

He and I felt that Wupatki, and the tower house, Wukoki, as well as the Citadel and the neighboring sites described by Fewkes in 1904, should come under the protection of the National Park Service. Mr. Clarke, working on the local level with the Flagstaff organizations, and I, through Dr. Fewkes and the Smithsonian, sponsored the executive order of President Coolidge establishing in 1924 the Wupatki National Monument.

Other authorities credit Mary-Russell (as well as Harold) with having a hand in the Wupatki project.

IN 1924, MARY-RUSSELL began to receive money from her mother's estate. A trust that had been created for Elise's benefit terminated upon her death and the proceeds, about $21,000 ($166,530 in 1997 dollars), came out of probate to Mary-Russell. In addition, Elise owned valuable property in her own right. After all estate taxes, expenses, and attorney's fees were paid, a check for $39,881 ($316,256) was sent to Mary-Russell. There were in addition a few minor sums realized from the sale of real estate and stock. In all, Mary-Russell realized about $70,000 ($555,100). Another trust remained in effect for the balance of Mary-Russell's life and paid her an annuity.

Harold immediately put the money to work for her in the E. W. Clark Company, the investment firm in which his father was a partner and which had successfully managed Harold's own portfolio for many years. Income from he inheritance in 1924 was $1,697 ($13,202). (Over the years it fluctuated, dwindling down to nothing during the Depression and coming back strongly after World War II.)

THE FOLLOWING YEAR, 1925, another milestone in the Colton family was reached when Harold's father succumbed to pneumonia on January 29, at the age of seventy-seven. The death meant that Harold inherited a considerable sum of money and that as the oldest male, he was head of the family. These circumstances led to his reconsidering of his life's direction. Harold did not enjoy teaching, though he was by this time a full professor of zoology. His salary in 1925 was $2,250 ($17,055), augmented by $30,422 ($236,683) from the securities portfolio given to him in 1909 by his father. An additional $22,000 ($166,760) came to him from new trusts created upon the death of his father, for a gross annual income of $70,052 ($530,994). He decided that the time had come to quit teaching and devote his life to his passionate interest in research and his newfound love of archaeology.

NOT LONG AFTER her father-in-law's death, Mary-Russell opened the exhibition for which she and Harold had been preparing since the summer of 1923. Titled "Aboriginal American Crafts," it included objects from Mary-Russell's collection and was well attended, receiving praise in the Philadelphia newspapers. Among the pieces on display was a bowl made by the Hopi potter

Nampeyo; the Coltons were among the first to recognize the value of Nampeyo's resurrection of ancient designs and her skill as an artist, and were early collectors of her work.

Harold, Mary-Russell, and Ferrell spent the summer of 1925 in Flagstaff, returning to the Babbitt pasture where they had stayed in 1923. Refitting their tents, they also added another dwelling, and Lewis and Cora Burnham joined them. Lewis wrote years later of that summer:

> *The big event of 1925 was our "circumnavigation" of the Grand Canyon by motor, over the dreaded dugway to the ferry at Lees Ferry, seeing Zion Park, and back via Las Vegas (no resemblance to the present town) and across the Colorado at Needles and home.*

It was during this stay that the Coltons realized how much they had come to love Flagstaff. One of the reasons that both Ferrell and Mary-Russell particularly enjoyed Flagstaff was that there at 7,000 feet in the clear mountain air, they had relief from health problems they suffered in Philadelphia, Ferrell with asthma and Mary-Russell with sinusitis. Ferrell's asthma was in fact so serious that he missed weeks of school when attacks hit him and was in danger of not being advanced with the rest of his class.

Mary-Russell and Harold began looking for a permanent summer homesite. After inspecting many possibilities, they decided that they liked the Babbitt property best. Harold bought the thirty-eight-acre parcel from C. J. Babbitt that summer, and made a gift of the land to Mary-Russell.

In addition to buying the Babbitt land, Harold made an offer to purchase the adjoining sixty acres from Nellie M. Francis, whose husband, Flagstaff pioneer John W. Francis, had recently died. The Francis land included a home and barn. Because the property was tied up in probate, Mrs. Francis was unable to give an immediate answer and the Coltons returned to the east without confirmed response. Nonetheless, they were in good spirits after another enjoyable Flagstaff summer.

Chapter Four

MAKING THE MOVE

MARY-RUSSELL FOUND herself as an artist in the Southwest. She experimented with new colors and techniques, and the change in her art was noticed. The Ten held their 1926 Philadelphia show from February 27 to March 20, and Mary-Russell entered four paintings. A newspaper reviewer said, "In the work of Mrs. Colton one feels an underlying sense of the grandeur of nature and the inconsequence of man." The show traveled, and she won a first prize for her oil, *Sunset and Moonglow,* depicting an Arizona scene, in Atlantic City.

IN THE SPRING of 1926, Mrs. Francis notified the Coltons that she had accepted their offer to buy her home and land in Flagstaff. Approval of the probate court for the sale of her deceased husband's interest in the property was obtained, and on April 10, 1926, a deed was issued, again in the name of Mary-Russell F. Colton, as a gift from Harold.

Combining the Francis property with the previously purchased Babbitt land meant that the Coltons now owned a choice one-hundred-acre tract of land north of Flagstaff covered with virgin pine forest and meadows. On it was situated a frame California-type bungalow, built by noted artist Louis Akin in 1911, which the Francis family called Malpais Manor. The Coltons thought that the name "manor" was pretentious, and changed it to Coyote Range.

Finally, after much discussion, the Coltons decided to cut their Philadelphia ties and move to Flagstaff. Although it was undoubtedly a hard decision because of their deep Eastern roots, they were not altogether unhappy to leave Singing Wood. The deaths there of three family members—Elise, Sabin, and Dysie—must have left a shadow on the home.

Leasing out Singing Wood, the Coltons drove to Flagstaff, bringing with them their dogs TayTay and Taku and shipping their furniture. Figuring that the furniture would travel slowly, they stopped en route for a short visit at the Pfefle Guest Ranch in Alcalde, New Mexico.

Upon arriving in Flagstaff, the newcomers stayed at their 1923 summer camp until they had done some work (primarily, remodeling the kitchen) on Coyote Range. They moved into their new home in the early summer.

At the camp site, they joined two of the shacks by building a living room between them; they called the place Sunrise House and used it to house their servants, Tom and Mary Higgins and the Higgins children. To complete the staff, they hired a cook and a housemaid. The Higgins family stayed in Flagstaff until 1930, when they moved back to Philadelphia. (Tom's mind mysteriously failed one night while he was with the Coltons on a camping trip on the Navajo Reservation during a storm. There was some speculation that he might have been struck by lightning.) The Coltons replaced him with J. D. Waldhaus, a distant relative of Harold's. (Waldhaus was in their employ from 1930 until 1935, when he left to become an active figure in local and state politics.)

In addition to getting their own dwellings in order, the Coltons brought Bug (whom Mary-Russell was now supporting) to Flagstaff, renting a duplex for her downtown. Within a year, Bug was taken to California by a friend who thought the Flagstaff altitude too high for Bug's health.

As new arrivals in Flagstaff, the Coltons spent time establishing themselves in town, finding out what was happening and who was who. A campaign to build a community hotel in Flagstaff opened just as the Coltons became residents, and Harold bought stock in it. The hotel was named the Monte Vista, and later played a role in the history of the Museum of Northern Arizona.

They also resumed their archaeological surveys. The *Coconino Sun* disclosed that Jesse Fewkes, a renowned archaeologist from the Smithsonian

Institution, was in Flagstaff conducting a sizable excavation of an Indian ruin. Front-page headlines were given to Fewkes, who spoke in such a way as to make readers believe that he had discovered the site. In fact, he was excavating the ruin that Mary-Russell had first found in October 1916. It was Fewkes who named the site Elden Pueblo; many significant finds were made at Elden Pueblo, all of them shipped to the Smithsonian. The Coltons introduced themselves to Fewkes, an important move in establishing themselves in archaeological circles, and had Fewkes as a dinner guest. (Harold had a low opinion of Fewkes, fueled perhaps by the fact that Fewkes tried to steal the credit for the discovery of Elden Pueblo from Mary-Russell.)

HAROLD AND MARY-RUSSELL had a treat in August 1926 when Lewis and Cora Burnham, with whom they had shared many adventures, visited them for a week. This was to be the first of many summer visits by family and friends. Summers in Philadelphia were insufferable, and with the move of Harold and Mary-Russell to cool Flagstaff, Coyote Range became an alternative to the family's traditional summer retreat in Maine. Blanche Shaw also visited Coyote Range that summer.

THE FRANCIS FAMILY had used Malpais Manor as a summer home, and upon their moving into it, the Coltons discovered this meant that the house was uninsulated and drafty and heated only with fireplaces. Flagstaff families who lived in such houses spent their winters in a warmer place, such as Phoenix or Southern California. The Coltons followed this example and lived during the winter OF 1926–27 in Redlands, California, where Harold's mother joined them for a time. The stay in Redlands paid an unexpected dividend: Ferrell's asthma disappeared completely there, never to trouble him again.

In April 1927, the Coltons returned to Flagstaff, and installed a central heating system in Coyote Range. Then they built a studio of native stone for Mary-Russell. The studio was located a couple of hundred yards south of the home, near the eastern bank of Schultz Creek, far enough away from the house so that she could work without disturbance. The setting was beautiful. Intended to be a place that would inspire her to paint, it served its purpose brilliantly.

Mary-Russell loved her studio and the woods surrounding it. She would often leave the studio in the evening and sit in a favorite place on the bank of Schultz Creek watching the play of light and shadow as the sun went down.

The Coltons built two other buildings on their property in 1927, an office for Harold and a guest cottage they called Bluejay House.

IN THE SPRING of 1927, the Coltons heard a rumor that a movie company was considering the purchase of the McMillan Ranch, a 318-acre tract located adjacent to their property on the north. Fearful that this might spoil the tranquillity and beauty of their homesite, Harold bought the property, and again, gave it to Mary-Russell.

The man who established the ranch, Thomas McMillan, was generally considered to have been Flagstaff's first settler, coming in 1876—before there was a town—with the tattered remnants of a flock of sheep that he brought from California to escape drought. Finding a flowing spring near a broad, grassy valley north of present-day Flagstaff, he located his sheep ranch at the site, which became the family homestead. During their long tenure, the McMillans had farmed the property, and had constructed a home, several barns, and other farm buildings on the land.

MARY-RUSSELL'S FRIEND and art-school classmate, Isabel Branson Cartwright, stayed with the Coltons at Bluejay House for a time that summer, which allowed Mary-Russell to find out what was happening in the Eastern art world. Isabel took this opportunity to paint a portrait of Mary-Russell.

Isabel Cartwright joined the family on one of their summer adventures. In order to broaden their knowledge of archaeology, the Coltons decided to go to New Mexico for the Pecos Conference being held there that summer. They had no invitation and felt like gate crashers, but believed that the potential for gain outweighed the risk of embarrassment. Traveling in their 1922 Buick, which was fitted for camping, they also took along Ferrell and his dog Gyp. On the way, the party stopped in Gallup to see the Indian Ceremonial.

When they arrived at Pecos, they found that the conference was a very informal affair. Most of the sessions were in the open air and consisted of scientists sitting around in a circle, discussing piles of potsherds or other

PORTRAIT OF MARY-RUSSELL BY HER ART SCHOOL FRIEND
ISABEL CARTWRIGHT, WHO WAS A GUEST IN THE COLTON HOUSE
IN FLAGSTAFF THAT SUMMER, 1927

interesting artifacts placed on the ground in front of them. The Coltons pitched a camp nearby and attended the sessions freely.

The host of the conference was famed archaeologist A. V. Kidder, who welcomed them. The Coltons enjoyed the conference and met a number of noted scientists, including Emil Haury, Earl Morris, Frank H. H. Roberts, Odd Halseth, Burton and Harriet Cosgrove, Paul S. Martin, and E. B. Renaud. These professionals were quite impressed to discover what the Coltons were doing in Flagstaff. Harold and Mary-Russell issued invitations to visit Coyote Range, which many of the attendees accepted; their relationships with some of these people ripened into close friendships. It was at this historic conference that the attendees adopted the Pecos Classification, a system of identifying prehistoric cultural eras by the nomenclature Basketmaker I to III and Pueblo I to V (this system continues to be widely used). Back home, Harold and Mary-Russell continued their search for Indian ruins, and made many trips into the country on horseback and by car, often camping overnight.

NOW THAT THE Coltons were residents of Flagstaff, they renewed their friendship with J. C. Clarke, with whom they had corresponded since 1921. Clarke had for years boosted the idea of a Flagstaff museum to house artifacts found in the area, and enlisted the support of the *Coconino Sun*. In 1924, he succeeded in establishing a small museum in a room in the Woman's Club building at 212 West Aspen Avenue. Clarke had written to the Coltons asking for money to buy shelving and display cases for the museum, and they had obliged.

By the time the Coltons moved to Flagstaff, the museum was an inactive nook graced only by a static display of dusty curios. The Coltons felt that the museum had potential and began to urge its expansion. At their prompting, a committee was created by the Chamber of Commerce to look into the idea.

The committee's first meeting on August 1, 1927, was followed by many others. There was much discussion about the scope of the museum. Some members wanted to limit its purpose to warehousing and displaying local artifacts. Several argued that it should be located on the campus of Arizona State Teachers College at Flagstaff, as an arm of the school, which would have been an inexpensive and convenient solution.

On August 12, 1927, Mary-Russell wrote a letter to the *Coconino Sun* stating her beliefs:

> *It has always been an understood thing that science and art are impractical, and yet business has not been able to do without the scientist, and where would the advertising man be today without the artist?*
>
> *And with this comforting thought I venture to put into words our thoughts on the museum matter.*
>
> *Flagstaff has at last an opportunity to show the effete east that she has taste and vision.*
>
> *The establishment of a museum of science and art, as a cultural and educational center, should go far toward the development of our little city.*
>
> *This is our "psychological moment." Will we look far enough ahead to envision the museum as a living, growing fact in the community, not only as a place for the storage and exhibition of archaeological material, but for the encouragement of modern and Indian art, so closely linked to the ancient, and*

as a unique setting for the exhibition of modern paintings, whose inspiration has been drawn from the deserts and canyons and picturesque native peoples of northern Arizona?

Surely a museum serving this threefold purpose would wield a far more extensive educational and cultural influence than a dead storage place for valuable material.

The desirability of the establishment of a museum for the care of our geological, zoological and archaeological treasures is acknowledged by all; but has the great educational value of a continuity between the ancient and modern native arts been thoroughly considered?

Our opportunity for this dual development is exceptional here, located as we are close to the Hopi and Navajo Indians whose people have instituted the very arts which we are about to go to so much pains to preserve today.

These peoples will soon have forgotten the secrets of their crafts, and when they vanish our country will have lost its only true native American art.

This is our chance to lend them a hand, as the Santa Fe museum has done for the Indians of the Rio Grande.

Encourage our Indians to produce only the best, using the beautiful old designs available in the museum, where they would bring their finest examples of modern Indian craftsmanship for exhibition and sale, side by side with the work of the ancient peoples.

Now this museum should be built, unit by unit, of native malpais rock and roofed with stout spruce timbers, somewhat after the pueblo style of architecture, and placed high upon a mesa top overlooking the city and facing the great Peaks; surely this would be appropriate to our magnificent setting here, and a tribute to the vision of our people

This would be something to build up to, as the intellectual apex of the town.

I see nothing in such a placement to hinder its use and inspiration to the young people of our college and our schools.

I hereby propose that we make our museum a unique asset to the town, its college and schools, and not merely a department of our normal college, which in itself is something to be proud of and can be expected to lead in all matters of intellectual good taste. . . .

Ultimately, the Coltons' views prevailed: the museum would feature both science and art and would be locally owned and independently operated. On December 16, 1927, the *Bylaws and Constitution of the Northern Arizona Society of Science and Art* were adopted. Mary-Russell and Harold were both incorporators.

With the creation of the new museum, ideas that had been turning in Mary-Russell's mind for months began to take shape, giving her life a new direction. She devised an ambitious program of action: She would teach art, bringing it into the lives of Flagstaff people. She would hold art exhibitions at the museum in order to introduce the community to beautiful things. She would hold art competitions in order to spur artists to create finer work, and give them the satisfaction of public appreciation. She would reward artists with cash prizes in order to stimulate them to participate. She would do something to rescue the dying Indian arts.

Their first full year in Flagstaff had been a productive one for Harold and Mary-Russell. With central heating installed in their home, the Coltons were able to stay at Coyote Range during the winter. By the end of 1927, they had become full-time Flagstaff residents.

IN 1928, MARY-RUSSELL began to farm the McMillan land, an avocation that occupied much of her time for sixteen years. As Harold later wrote:

> *Mary-Russell with plantation ancestors [the Polks of Tennessee] naturally took over the management of the ranch. I hired a farmer, Charles Priest and built him a two-bedroom farm house, which we appropriately called the "Rectory."*

Although she may have had plantation ancestors, Mary-Russell lacked any direct experience with agriculture. Rather, she was a "mail-order" farmer, accumulating her knowledge through books and magazines. She had the good sense also to consult with knowledgeable people and to hire men who had had experience farming at Flagstaff's 7,000-foot elevation. The soil was rich in minerals, and healthy, but scant rainfall and a short growing season made farming difficult and chancy.

Over the years, the Coltons hired a number of people to work on the farm. The hired farmers did the heavy work while Mary-Russell did the planning and management. In addition to the farm, Mary-Russell had a flower and vegetable garden near the house, which she personally tended, although here too, hired hands did the heavy work such as plowing and hoeing. The home garden was the only plot that was watered, while the other crops were dry-farmed.

In addition to growing crops, Mary-Russell had a deep love of animals, and raised many different kinds. She was especially fond of chickens, and seemed always to have at least a few on hand. At times she had hundreds. For a while she kept a cow in the barn and went there every day to milk and to make a soft white cheese. In addition to these domesticated animals, Coyote Range was visited by many wild creatures. Animals instinctively trusted Mary-Russell and she tamed several wild deer and even a family of porcupines.

IN ADDITION TO farming the McMillan property, the Coltons set about making improvements to the old McMillan home. It had potential, but required refurbishing and modernization to make it livable. Harold described it:

> *The house had no foundation but rested on a few large boulders. When the snow melted in March a river ran under the building among the boulders. The house had been built in 1886. We called it the Homestead. It had a parlor, dining room and bedroom on the first floor and four bedrooms and an attic on the second floor. Thomas McMillan, Jr. was raising chickens in the second story front bedroom when I bought it. We put in a masonry foundation and a new roof.*

ON MAY 21, 1928, the first Board of Trustees of the Northern Arizona Society of Science and Art was chosen. It was a distinguished group, and by serving on it, Harold and Mary-Russell not only furthered the interests of the museum, but came to know these community leaders well. Several of them became close friends.

The board elected Harold as its president and director and selected a name for the new institution. Once the museum was organized, Mary-Russell and Harold immediately went to work to see that it became a lively institution. It did not take long before the Coltons assumed the day-to-day operation of the museum and it became, in effect, their personal enterprise. Mary-Russell was appointed the curator of art and organized the museum's arts and crafts section.

As a result of the stir caused by the creation of the museum, townspeople were energized and artifacts began to pour in. The Coltons themselves made several significant gifts from their many summers of exploration. As reported in the newspaper, these included, "Five axe-heads from Picture Canyon which were discovered under some debris in an ancient dwelling by Mrs. Colton while they were eating lunch." More room was taken in the Woman's Club building to house the collections. In July 1928, Mary-Russell and Harold began a publication for the new institution, called *Museum Notes* (renamed *Plateau* in 1939).

Mary-Russell, though by temperament not a joiner, became a member of the Shakespeare Club and the Flagstaff Woman's Club and eventually was elected to the board of trustees of the latter. A feature of both of her clubs was that they met on a rotating basis at the homes of their members. Mary-Russell duly took part, acting as hostess on several occasions.

Neither was a regular churchgoer in Flagstaff. Harold, of a scientific mind even when he was a child, turned his investigative methods to religion when he was a young man. When his Mendellian studies on the Old Testament's list of "begats" showed obvious lapses and flaws, he became a skeptic, if not an outright atheist. Mary-Russell was confirmed in the Episcopal church in 1906 and remained a spiritual person all her life, but as an adult seldom attended services, although both she and Harold went to the Episcopal church in Flagstaff on special occasions.

Mary-Russell came into town occasionally to shop or take care of other matters. She did not drive, so going to town meant getting one of the employees to act as chauffeur, no doubt giving some townspeople the idea that she was putting on airs and playing the fine lady. Harold, who to the contrary liked to drive, was fairly often seen on the streets of Flagstaff, and was considered to be more of a regular fellow. Some Flagstaff residents inferred that Mary-Russell was a snob or considered herself superior. She harbored no such thoughts. Her son Ferrell observed that she was friendly and liked the women of Flagstaff, but was simply in a position where she didn't drive, lived some distance from town, and was engrossed in museum activities, leaving little time to socialize beyond her club meetings.

AS THE MUSEUM began its new life, the contacts Harold and Mary-Russell had made with "Southwesterners" at the Pecos Conference and other archaeological meetings began to yield fruit. Scientists coming to Flagstaff used the museum and the Colton home as a base of operations. Mary-Russell was hostess to a growing stream of visiting scientists. The family met many interesting people this way, some of whom became lifelong friends.

Mary-Russell was indefatigable in her role as a founder and organizer of the museum, throwing herself whole-heartedly into the work of the new institution. After forming her section and announcing her plans, the first thing to which she turned her attention was bringing art to Flagstaff. She announced that she would teach art, her belief being that "art education is not a mere cultural frill, but a basic necessity." The Woman's Club building had no room for art classes, so Mary-Russell arranged for space in the high-school building for an art studio. She held her first exhibition on August 2, 1928, at Flagstaff High School and began giving art lessons there. She also began to bring exhibitions of high-quality art to Flagstaff and to assemble a fine-arts collection for the museum.

Having established a program for the townspeople, Mary-Russell next turned her attention to the sad state of Indian arts and crafts, about which she wrote:

> We believed that our first duty lay with our native population, the Indians of the Painted Desert, our next door neighbors. We were rather well fitted for this work, having traveled about among the people for years on painting and archaeological trips, and for years having watched with deep regret a gradual degeneration of their unique arts and crafts.

She conducted a study and found that the Hopis had at one time made over seventy types of craft objects, more than any other tribe, but that many of their crafts were in decline and were being replaced by cheap machine-made imitations.

In the fall of 1928, Mary-Russell began to work in earnest on a plan to rescue Hopi arts and crafts. From her own experience she knew the importance to artists of being able to sell their work, saying:

> It is a generally accepted fact that even the artist must eat! True, there is a literary fallacy to the effect that the hungry genius produces the really inspired work of art, but take it from an old painter, three meals a day [are] stimulating to genius.

She decided to sponsor a Hopi arts and crafts exhibition at the museum, believing such an exhibition would not only provide a marketplace, but that she could encourage the production of works of artistic merit by judging the entries and awarding prizes.

Mary-Russell explained in an unpublished manuscript why she selected the Hopis: "The Hopi were chosen, because they have never received any attention from any other source & represent a group of very ancient & important arts practiced by a town dwelling stationary group which the museum felt qualified to handle in an intensive manner."

As the format for a Hopi arts and crafts exhibition was taking shape in her mind, she realized that it would be a major undertaking and that conditions were not yet right at home or at the museum to begin it.

EIGHT DAYS BEFORE Christmas 1928, the Coltons' house burned to the ground. The fire started in the attic and quickly engulfed the structure. Mary-Russell's outside studio was undamaged by the fire, and most of her art work was saved, with the exception of four paintings in the house. Harold lost a valuable scientific library, but because he stored the bulk of his scientific papers in his outside office, they also were spared. Both lost a great many personal effects, including family heirlooms and memorabilia. It was a sad close to an otherwise satisfying year.

The people of Flagstaff came forward to help the Coltons recover from the fire, though little could be done. The family moved into the Monte Vista Hotel in downtown Flagstaff for a few days, then spent Christmas at Phantom Ranch in the bottom of the Grand Canyon, while they had Bluejay House made ready for occupancy upon their return.

The fire made building a new home the first priority in the lives of the

Coltons, but Mary-Russell did not neglect her self-imposed duties at the museum. In January 1929, she announced that she would present three traveling shows arranged through the American Federation of Arts, and would give lectures in connection with two of them. In addition, she announced that the museum would hold evening art classes for the public.

On the heels of this announcement, the board of directors of the museum held its first annual meeting. It was revealed that a gift of $2,500 ($19,400) had been given to the museum by an anonymous donor, though the newspaper reported this with a wink, for everyone knew that the Coltons had provided the money. With the gift added to membership dues, the fledgling museum was solidly in the black.

By the spring of 1929, the Museum of Northern Arizona had outgrown the space originally allotted to it. In April, Mary-Russell entered into negotiations with the members of the governing board of the Woman's Club. The club was having difficulty making payments on its mortgage, and when Mary-Russell offered to rent the entire building for the museum, the club gladly accepted the offer.

IN PLANNING THE new Coyote Range, Mary-Russell and Harold had an idea of the kind of home they wanted. Harold, who had had some architectural training, drew rough plans. They then contacted Harold's brother Ralph, a certified Philadelphia architect, to finish them.

Both Harold and Mary-Russell had been charmed by the Spanish mission style of architecture that they had seen in Santa Fe. They met Ralph and his wife, Florence, in Santa Fe and toured the area, getting ideas; this was followed by a visit to Flagstaff to show Ralph the site. They then looked at Spanish- and Mission-style homes in Phoenix and Tucson. Ralph took their ideas and sketches and added his own inspirations and refinements upon returning to his office. He prepared a set of tentative plans and sent them to the Coltons, who suggested some revisions and additions. Correspondence went back and forth until the final plans were approved in May 1929. Construction began soon afterward. As much as possible, native materials gathered in the vicinity were used to build the home.

At almost the same time they started construction, they found a buyer for

Singing Wood and sold it for $66,783 ($518,236). Their timing was fortunate: a few months later, the stock-market crash of 1929 devalued such properties by many thousands of dollars. The Singing Wood sales money, together with the fire insurance proceeds, was enough to build and furnish the new Coyote Range. While the construction workers were on the premises, the Coltons had them build an addition to Mary-Russell's art studio.

The Coltons, in search of help for Mary-Russell in her Hopi projects, heard of Edmund Nequatewa, and wrote him a letter, inviting him to contact them. He responded, paying them a visit. They hit it off and in early April 1929, Nequatewa began a long association with the Coltons, working at first as a gardener and caretaker of the turkeys and chickens.

BY THIS TIME, Harold and Mary-Russell, though newcomers to South-western studies, had established a reputation for expertise in Indian affairs, and were appointed by Arizona Senator Carl Hayden to participate in a study of federal facilities on Indian reservations in Arizona. They toured the Indian agency office and school at Tuba City, then went to the sanitorium at Kayenta. They and the other members of the commission spent five days in the endeavor, and made a written report of their findings, which was published in the records of the United States Senate.

The Coltons attended the conference of the American Association for the Advancement of Science held in Albuquerque in April, where Mary-Russell presented a paper about Hopi art. The Coltons traveled by car, spending two days on the road each way. On the alert for ruin sites en route, they discovered twenty-five of them.

The Coltons attended another scientific convention that year, the second edition of the Pecos Conference. Like the first, it was actually held at Pecos, New Mexico, and was informal, with many outdoor sessions. They took their car and camped at the site again, with Thomas Higgins and their cook. At the end of the conference, Harold and Mary-Russell joined Dr. E. B. Renaud of Denver University and toured the Four Corners area, taking in Mesa Verde, Bluff, and Kayenta, searching for archaeological sites. One of Renaud's student assistants at Denver University was Katharine Bartlett, who took a summer job at the museum as a result of this contact.

THAT SUMMER, MARY-RUSSELL inaugurated an event that became an annual feature, the Exhibition of Arizona Artists, which was open to amateurs and professionals alike. It was held July 8 to 29, 1929, and she got it off to a rousing start by hosting a tea at which she boosted the idea of Flagstaff as a cultural hub equal to New Mexico's Taos and Santa Fe:

New Mexico has its Taos artist colony and Santa Fe is a mecca for painters and artist folk from all over the country. Flagstaff has the same possibilities through its location in the center of a wonderful region and should become a lodestone from all over the United States. . . . To make this possible . . . , we must create an atmosphere for painters, a center of interest must be established, and one of the best ways of doing this is to hold frequent exhibitions and to do everything to make the artists of our state and those who visit our city feel that our Museum is their natural headquarters. . . .

Sixteen exhibitors displayed thirty-two entries in a variety of arts and crafts. Mary-Russell showed three of her own oils, *Desert Range, In the Valley of the Painted Hills* (plate 7), and *A California Valley.* The latter two were the paintings that she sent to The Ten for its show in February 1929. They had already been reviewed favorably in major newspapers in the East and must have set a high tone for the Flagstaff event.

Later that summer, Mary-Russell sponsored an exhibition of art by Indian children from the Tuba City schools. This exhibition was the forerunner of the Junior Art Show.

IN OCTOBER 1929, Harold, Mary-Russell, and Ferrell visited the East for several weeks. Harold went to Washington and Mary-Russell re-established her contacts with people in the art field. She also attended the second 1929 show of The Ten, held November 9 to December 1 in Philadelphia, where she had five paintings. The exhibition was so successful that it was also booked into Washington, D. C.

Upon their return to Flagstaff late in November, the Coltons found that work on Coyote Range had gone well. The construction was right on schedule and it seemed certain that they would be able to move in at the beginning of 1930. They spent the balance of the winter in Tucson. While the house was under construction, a reporter for the *Coconino Sun* paid it a visit. After giving a very detailed description of the dwelling, the writer summed it up:

> *It is simple, but princely, reflecting the very best of taste, and implying that cost was no object in attaining what that taste demanded. It is one of the show places of the west and while Dr. and Mrs. Colton do not expect to place it upon exhibition, they say they will be pleased to have everyone in Flagstaff drive out and look it over.*

MARY-RUSSELL BEGAN her career as a benefactor to the Hopis at Christmas 1929 with a generous contribution of presents, which included cash as well as other things. The money was appreciated and went a long way on the reservation. Some gifts met specific needs, such as four rocking chairs and a "nice lot of curtain material" that she sent to the Indian Field Service at Kayenta. Mary-Russell donated her hand-me-down clothing and shoes to the Hopis as well. Thereafter, she never failed to give them Christmas presents, and over the years, her giving touched the lives of many. She also began to support an old couple who had been servants of the Houston family in Louisville, Mr. and Mrs. Alex McEuen. The end of the year found Mary-Russell poised to begin yet another phase of her life.

Chapter Five

FULL FLOWERING

THE 1930S WERE Mary-Russell's most productive years, the time when she produced her best paintings and made invaluable contributions to the revival and preservation of Hopi art. It was as though much of her life had been spent in preparation for this decade.

ON JANUARY 11, 1930, the Coltons moved into their new home, after having it blessed by a Hopi priest, who placed a *paho* (prayer stick) in the ceiling beam. After they were settled in, Mary-Russell launched into her art enterprises with fresh zeal. In addition to her existing activities, she decided that the time had come to begin work on her goal of reviving Indian arts and crafts.

She began her effort by compiling a list of five areas in which she felt she could help:

1. Cotton textiles: Hopi textiles had traditionally been of the highest quality and were avidly sought by neighboring tribes as trade items. In modern times, however, the Hopis had stopped growing their own cotton and, instead, bought spools of ordinary kitchen twine and used it to make their textiles. This resulted in a thin, shiny, unattractive, and flimsy product. Mary-Russell planned to obtain good-quality, long staple cotton and sell it at cost to the Hopi weavers. (Of all the Hopi arts, weaving was Mary-Russell's favorite.)

INTERIOR OF COYOTE RANGE, 1930

2. Indigo: The Hopis had for many years used and loved a deep blue dye made from indigo, a plant originally grown in India but later transplanted to Mexico. Trading post operators had carried this product as a standard item of inventory, but when it became difficult to find, they switched to chemical dyes. Mary-Russell determined to find a source of genuine indigo and make it available to the Hopis at cost.

3. Vegetable dyes: As with indigo, a whole range of native Hopi dyes had been supplanted by chemical dyes, used both in textiles and basketry. These often produced a garish and non-traditional result, quite spoiling the look of some crafts. Mary-Russell decided to embark upon a study of native dye plants and materials, and to preserve the knowledge.

4. Pottery: Mary-Russell felt that this was the most debased of all the Hopi arts and that it had fallen farthest from grace. The walls of the pots were of unequal thickness, firing was uneven, and the paint was indifferently applied, often rubbing off the finished pieces. She vowed to conduct experiments with firing techniques and paints.

5. Woolen textiles: Mary-Russell believed that the Merino sheep

breed—introduced by federal agents—produced an unsuitable wool. Merino wool was short, had a sharp crimp, and was greasy. She planned to research and experiment to find a better breed. In this connection, she learned how to card and spin the native wool. Mary-Russell expressed her philosophy about the problem in her article, "The Hopi Craftsman" published in the July 1930 issue of *Museum Notes:*

The art of a people is only of value in so long as it maintains a distinct pure bred character. Like all native people in the process of readjustment, their art has a tendency to absorb the worst rather than the best, from the dominant civilization that has surrounded them. It behooves this dominant civilization to lend every assistance and encouragement to its native people to maintain the purity of its beautiful peasant arts and bring with it a worthy contribution to the new era.

Having determined her agenda, Mary-Russell—with enthusiastic support from Harold—became a woman with a mission, one that was to consume a substantial part of her life and yield important and lasting results.

In the spring of 1930, she decided to test her idea for a Hopi Craftsman Exhibition. She knew that she and Harold would have to make many arrangements if it were to succeed. Acknowledging the influence that Bureau of Indian Affairs officials had in Indian matters, they first sought the blessing of the federal agents in charge of the Hopi jurisdiction. They started at the top, in Washington, D.C., and in March, obtained the approval of Charles Rhoads, Commissioner of Indian Affairs. Then they went to the local level, and as Harold described it, "The agent, Mr. Miller, reluctantly O.K.ed our project. [To him] it was just one of those things that 'do-gooders' think up."

With federal approval in hand, Mary-Russell invented the basic format for the show. It was so well thought-out that it was followed for many years:

1. The Hopi Craftsman Exhibition would be held around the Fourth of July, when the weather was fine, Flagstaff held other celebrations, and many visitors were in town.

2. She and Harold would visit the reservation in May and June to obtain the goods for the show.

3. Mary-Russell would examine the offered items in the villages and decide on the spot that had enough merit for the exhibition.

4. The museum would give the makers a receipt for all goods accepted and would transport them to Flagstaff free of shipping charges. The museum would pay for any damage to the goods in transit or while on display.

5. The goods would be exhibited and offered for sale at prices fixed by the artists.

6. The museum would advertise the exhibition and make a concerted effort to have good attendance in order to enhance the possibilities for selling the merchandise.

7. The museum itself might buy pieces.

8. The goods would be judged at the museum and prizes would be awarded for the best items in various categories. (Mary-Russell was so committed to the project that she herself provided the prize money from her own funds.)

9. After each individual piece was judged, the goods would be reassembled by village, so that there was competition among the villages to do the best work and receive the most prizes.

10. Selected Hopi craftsmen would perform live demonstrations of their skills at the exhibition. (Mary-Russell believed that "There is no exhibit so effective as a live working demonstration.")

11. After the exhibition, the unsold goods would be packed for return to the reservation. An accounting would be made for the sold items, and the sales proceeds and the prize money would be taken with the unsold goods back to the reservation and given to the owners.

12. No commission or expenses of any kind would be charged by the museum—all of its work was free.

13. There would be a follow-up visit by the Coltons to the Hopi mesas in the fall to talk to the artisans, explain why prizes had been awarded, stimulate certain crafts and techniques, and build good will.

This was an attractive program, one in which the Hopi artists had everything to gain and nothing to lose. The next step was to explain the idea to the Hopis and convince them to participate.

On March 19, 1930, Mary-Russell and Harold made their first approach to the Hopis. They took museum employees Edmund Nequatewa and Lyndon Hargrave on the trip. Nequatewa was well educated and fluent in both Hopi and English. He was able to introduce the members of the party to reservation dwellers and act as translator.

Any trip to the reservation in those days was an ordeal. As Mary-Russell explained later: "All [the mesas are] located some eighty miles or so from Flagstaff and reached over extremely bad roads. These roads are frequently impassable during the rainy season which commences early in July and continues until late in August."

They went to the reservation via Leupp, driving their old station wagon, Petie. The trip took several days and there were no lodgings along the way, so the party set up camps, where "Mary-Russell would cook our supper over an open fire and we would sleep on the ground or in the car. At dawn we were up, Mary-Russell cooked the breakfast which included all that was not eaten at supper, which was usually not much," Harold recalled. They had to get into the villages early to catch the men before they went to work in the fields.

The first morning they climbed the trail to the village of Shungopavi by foot, where Edmund explained the reason for their coming to the Hopis, who listened politely but were noncommittal. One of the first artisans to announce support for the idea was Sequoptewa, a weaver. He also agreed to be a demonstrator. The chief of Moenkopi, who was a friend of the Coltons, happened to be in Shungopavi at the time. He thought the Hopi Craftsman Exhibition was a good idea and enthusiastically argued in its favor to the people of Shungopavi for over an hour. Though he was not the chief of their village, he was a respected man and his support carried great weight.

Then the Colton party spent a week going from village to village "laboriously spreading information about the exhibition." They were received cordially and the Hopis listened to them with respect, but Harold and Mary-Russell could not know whether the idea would succeed until the time came for the Hopis to actually trust them with their goods. Most of the Hopi arts and crafts were produced during the winter when farming and livestock activities were in a lull. The crafts were important to the families, who depended on them to provide a vitally needed supplement to the income they received from farming and stock raising. To entrust their entire winter's production to the Coltons for the first Hopi Craftsman Exhibition—an untried event however good its sponsors' intentions—would be an act of faith.

The Coltons met resistance from only one person, Lorenzo Hubbell, Jr., who, they believed, feared that the Hopi Craftsman Exhibition might cost him some business. The Coltons felt he was concerned that if the they raised the standard of Hopi art work, it would cause tourists to demand high-quality merchandise and Hubbell would be unable to sell the cheap goods he had on hand.

The Coltons returned to Flagstaff on March 24, hopeful but knowing that the project might fail.

Two months later, the Coltons visited the Hopi villages with two trucks, crates, barrels, and packing materials. They visited all twelve pueblos, collecting goods for the show. The trip was painstaking and took them a week.

The first collecting visit proved to be a good one, as the Hopis turned over many beautiful wares. The chief of Shipaulovi, where the people had previously been reluctant to cooperate, saw the contributions that were pouring in from other villages. In order that his people not be outdone, he went house-to-house in his own village, gathering goods. Eventually two truck loads were assembled.

IT WAS AFTER this first collecting trip that Katharine Bartlett returned to the museum. She was a young anthropologist, just finishing her master's degree at the University of Denver. A short-stay visitor at the museum in 1929, she came back in 1930 to catalog a collection of artifacts. She so impressed the Coltons that they hired her as a permanent staff member. Katharine remained an employee of the museum for over sixty years, a versatile and untiring asset. She went on all of the trips to the Hopi mesas with the Coltons over the years, and had charge of tagging and accounting for all of the items submitted by the Hopi artists. (She eventually moved in with the Coltons, coming as a boarder but treated like one of the family.)

Katharine Bartlett wrote a memoir in 1990 describing a "day in the life" at the Colton house during the thirties, when the Coltons always had household help. Early in the decade the employees were Filipinos, but these were later replaced by two young Hopi girls, who "learned quickly and looked very cute in the pretty uniforms Mary-Russell ordered for them." When breakfast was finished, Harold walked across the driveway to his office, pausing to check his weather gauges and stock his bird feeders. Mary-Russell would "plan the meals for the day, direct the help and several times each week be driven to Flagstaff to the market to buy food and do whatever other shopping she had." If Mary-Russell did not go to town, she might garden or take care of farm management. At times she went to the museum and dealt with art projects. She did much of her painting in her studio in the winter, after the gardening and farming had ceased. Lunch was served at 12:30 and a large bell was rung to announce it. Dinner was usually a light meal. After dinner, the family would go to the movies at the Orpheum Theatre downtown or retire to the living room to read. Harold read everything from scientific journals to fiction. He loved the classics and would sometimes read Dickens out loud. Mary-Russell usually read art magazines, *Life,* or the *Saturday Evening Post.* Harold loved to listen to the radio and would regularly tune in to his favorite shows, which included comedy programs such as *The Great Gildersleeve* or *Fibber McGee and Molly.*

Sometimes the family would go on an outing. This could be just a pleasure picnic or some kind of museum business, such as an excavation. Mary-Russell would take along her painting kit. If she found a good subject, she would paint. Otherwise, she would just enjoy being out. The family turned all of these picnics into field trips, as they dearly loved roaming about.

Harold, who had been brought up in a large and outgoing family, loved to entertain and to have friends in for dinner. Mary-Russell, with her more solitary background, was shy about this, but rose to the challenge and was always a gracious hostess, "and planned delicious meals served on a beautifully appointed table."

ANOTHER IMPORTANT ADDITION to the staff in 1930 was Jimmie Kewanwytewa, known fondly as Jimmie K. He, like Edmund Nequatewa, was a bilingual Hopi who proved very helpful as an interpreter and as one who

PLATE 1. *Three Horses,* pencil, 15½ by 18½ inches, 1902. Collection of the Museum of Northern Arizona.

PLATE 2. *Portrait of Julia McMahon,* charcoal, 29½ by 22 inches, 1911. Collection of the Museum of Northern Arizona.

PLATE 3. *Church at Ranchos de Taos*, watercolor, 22 by 27 inches, 1913–1914. Collection of the Museum of Northern Arizona.

PLATE 4. *Walpi*, oil, 36 by 53 inches, 1914. Collection of the Museum of Northern Arizona.

PLATE 5. *Navajo Shepherdess*, oil, 36 by 26 inches, 1918. Collection of the Museum of Northern Arizona.

PLATE 6. *Afternoon Sandstorm in the Painted Desert*, oil, 27 by 30 inches, 1925. Collection of J. Ferrell Colton; photograph courtesy of Melchor Ruiz.

PLATE 7. *In the Valley of the Painted Hills*, oil, 31½ by 41½ inches, 1928. Collection of the Museum of Northern Arizona.

PLATE 8. *Hart Prairie*,
oil, 30 by 24 inches, 1930.
Collection of the Museum
of Northern Arizona.

PLATE 9. *Sequaptewa*,
gesso on plaster, 20
by 26 inches, 1931.
Collection of the
Museum of Northern
Arizona.

PLATE 10. *Smith Mountain, British Columbia*, oil, 25½ by 36 inches, 1910. Collection of Elise B. Colton; photograph courtesy of Melchor Ruiz.

PLATE 11. *Canyon de Chelly*, Arizona, oil, 27 by 30 inches, 1913–20. Collection of Jean Wilson.

PLATE 12. *Edmund Nequatewa*, gesso and oil on wood, 32 by 42 inches, 1942. Collection of the Museum of Northern Arizona.

PLATE 13. *San Francisco Peaks*, oil, 25 by 30 inches, 1929. Collection of Richard and Jean Wilson.

PLATE 14. *Red Rock Country*, oil, 27 by 36 inches, 1919. Collection of Elise B. Colton; photograph courtesy of Melchor Ruiz.

could explain Hopi ways. Though hired as a custodian, he was a jack-of-all-trades and no mean craftsman himself, noted for fine kachinas. When Mary-Russell saw that Jimmie and his kachina-carving friends did not sign their kachinas nor identify the figures with any kind of maker's mark, she showed him how she and other artists signed paintings. She convinced him to begin signing his kachinas, a practice that soon became universal with Hopi carvers, as it added to the value of the figures and established reputations for their makers.

NEAR THE END of June 1930, just before the Hopi Craftsman Exhibition, Harold and Mary-Russell made a final collecting trip to the reservation. It was the last chance for the Hopis who wanted to participate, and some of the craftsmen who had been reluctant to contribute now came forward. The Coltons drove away with even more goods.

At the museum, which had limited space, Mary-Russell devised an attractive layout for the exhibition, with the arts and crafts on display along the side walls of the main room and demonstrations at the ends. The live demonstrations were an inspired idea and became one of the most popular features of the shows. As Harold later described it:

> Certain of the craftsmen had volunteered their aid as demonstrators and appeared in holiday attire. A Hopi weaver set up his loom on the museum stage. A basket maker from Oraibi demonstrated her method of making reed baskets and plaques, and a Second Mesa woman from Shungopovi fashioned a beautiful coiled basket while a potter from Sichomivi completed the picture.

Mary-Russell did the final judging of the arts and crafts at the museum, and since there were scores of items, this was a Herculean task. She also awarded the prizes and then grouped the goods by village.

The Coltons had advertised the Hopi Craftsman Exhibition by every means they could think of, and hoped for good attendance. They had a good stock of quality items and the demonstrators were ready to perform. Still, in spite of all the hard work and expense needed to get the show ready, no one knew how the public would react.

By opening day, July 2, 1930, the Coltons were able to put their fears of failure aside. As Harold put it,

Indians swarmed in from the Reservation. The Assistant Commissioner of Indian Affairs dropped in from Washington. Then the dry season broke with a gentle rain, which was interpreted to mean that the benevolent Kachinas that dwell in the towering Peaks above the town, were pleased. It was, therefore, a huge success.

Tallies showed that one thousand people attended the first Hopi Craftsman Exhibition, including visitors from Germany and Czechoslovakia. The value of Mary-Russell's idea was confirmed. "It [was] a monument to [Mary-Russell's] powers of organization and dedication," Harold said later.

After the exhibition, the staff packed the unsold goods and prepared to return them to the makers, along with prize and sales money. Getting payment to the Hopis was difficult. The Coltons did not want to carry cash, and as there were no banks on the reservation, writing checks was impractical. There was, however, a post office, so the most feasible method of payment turned out to be postal money orders. Katharine hurried to the post office and purchased money orders to pay the Hopis their prize and sales money, and the Coltons returned to the reservation. In some ways, this final trip was the most important of all, for it established the essential bond of trust, proving to the Hopis that the Coltons would keep their promises.

In addition to this "business" trip, the Coltons made yet another trip in the fall. It served a different purpose, as explained by Mary-Russell:

[A] trip is made in September by Dr. Colton and myself when I spend a week or so visiting practically every worker in the twelve villages individually and discussing with them the reasons for the awards which have been made during the exhibition. At this time work for the coming winter is talked over; market problems are discussed; possible improvements in the various types of work are discussed with the craftsmen and demonstrations are used wherever possible, such as cases of vegetable dyes, wool exhibits, etc.

Mary-Russell herself purchased a number of prize-winning pieces that appeared at this first exhibition on behalf of the museum. Later, she assembled them into a traveling collection and sent it to the Indian Arts Fair in Santa Fe and to the Arizona State Fair.

The first Hopi Craftsman Exhibition—by long odds the hardest work that the museum had ever done—was a success. It remained to be seen whether it would have a lasting beneficial impact on the revival and preservation of the traditional goods and techniques of the Hopis. It also committed the Coltons to years of difficult work and the expenditure of considerable sums of money.

Hard on the heels of the Hopi show, Mary-Russell plunged into other art-related activity. She hosted the second annual Exhibition of Arizona Artists, July 19 to August 9, in which twenty-eight artists presented fifty-four exhibits; Mary-Russell contributed $110 ($875) as prize money. Several members of the Tucson Palette and Brush Club sent canvases, a result of Mary-Russell's visit the preceding fall. She also staged five other exhibitions in 1930, including a display of homemade Christmas cards, which she made an annual event. In between, she managed to attend the meeting of the American Federation of the Arts in Santa Fe.

Later that summer, Mary-Russell assembled a traveling exhibit of Hopi and Navajo art, entitled "Craftsmen of the Painted Desert," with the help of Indian trader Lorenzo Hubbell, Jr. This was sent to schools and museums all over the country. To accompany the traveling exhibit, she wrote a paper explaining Navajo and Hopi customs and their methods of producing arts and crafts.

It was during this time that Mary-Russell made a discovery that was to rejuvenate her own painting. In art school, she had been taught to prepare a canvas by underpainting it with umber. This gave the finished painting a dark, somber tone. In her reading, she came across the old gesso technique, which used an underpainting of specially prepared plaster of paris. This acted the opposite of umber, giving a shimmering brilliance to paint laid on top of it. Gesso was just right for the scenes of her new world, the glowing sunsets, rainbows on the Painted Desert, and dancing aspen leaves. Once she began employing this technique, her work took on a new look and she was energized and inspired.

IN SPITE OF all of her other activities that almost unbelievably busy summer, Mary-Russell found time to garden. In the September Flagstaff flower show, she won first prize for the most artistic floral arrangement. She entered grains and vegetables in the third annual Coconino County Fair held in October and walked away with many prizes, including the sweepstakes for mountain-district gardening. She entered poultry, winning prizes there as well. Moving upward from the county level, she entered some of her best produce in the Arizona State Fair in November and won prizes for her rye, oats, and wheat.

IN OCTOBER 1930, Mary-Russell began work to obtain long staple cotton for Hopi weaving. She searched fruitlessly until she was put in touch with the Arizona Industrial Congress. She wrote to its director on October 14, "We find that the traders do not carry cotton of a proper quality for the weavers' use in the making of hand-spun cotton textiles. Please let me know where we can get long staple cotton for them." She sent along a sample of the string that the Hopi weavers were using at the time.

The inquiry was routed to cotton brokers Peek and Fleming, who responded that while they were willing to help, they only dealt with large volumes, more than Mary-Russell would want to buy. This problem was solved, however, when it turned out that the brokers routinely pulled samples from each bale and saved those samples in hundred-pound bags, a workable amount.

On October 22, 1930, Mary-Russell ordered one hundred pounds of the cotton, earmarking forty pounds for Lorenzo Hubbell, Jr., another forty pounds for Tom Pavatea, and the remaining twenty pounds for herself. The same day, she wrote Hubbell and Pavatea:

> You will be surprised to receive very soon, forty pounds of long staple Pima cotton from Phoenix. . . . I am pleased to present you with forty pounds of this cotton, if you will distribute it without charge among the weavers. However, if you think best you can pay me for it and sell it at your discretion.

When the traders declined to stock the cotton, Mary-Russell, who believed strongly in the worth of her idea, sold the cotton directly from the museum, generally by mail order and always at cost. Although this added a burden to her already considerable list of duties, she made the cotton available this way for many years.

This same year, Mary-Russell began work on another of the items on her agenda, the study of native Hopi dyes. The knowledge of suitable materials and how to employ them was fading as death carried away the old Hopis, the last generation to have used native dyes. The young artisans were already using chemical dyes, which were cheap and handy. Mary-Russell asked the Hopis endless questions about plants and other materials that could produce dyes, located and collected samples, and made copious field notes.

In order to test the information she was gathering, she set up a little laboratory in an extra room in her studio and began experiments. It was not enough for her to know that a certain plant would produce a brilliant red. It was also necessary to know how to extract the active substances and to fix them so that they would be colorfast, using materials available to the Hopis. This required her to do such things as boiling weeds in sheep urine. Once she was satisfied that she had produced a reliable and reproducible result, she wrote down the recipe and filed it. Her work resulted in a wall filled with mason jars containing herbs, minerals, and other colorful substances.

On November 13, 1930, the Coltons went by train to the East Coast. They took Harold's mother, who had been visiting them, home and spent time around Philadelphia, renewing friendships. As *Museum Notes* suggested in its report of 1930 museum activities, its curator of art had been "exceedingly active."

IN MAY 1931, Mary-Russell hosted the first Junior Art Show. This was a bold addition to the considerable work already required for the Hopi Craftsman and Arizona Artists exhibitions. In launching the new program, she issued a press release stating her vision for the show:

Art education must begin with children. We must grow our own artists. The material is here awaiting encouragement and cultivation.

All about us is great beauty, grandeur of form, glory of color, sweep of opalescent desert, dark forests and snow capped peaks. Nowhere in the world has man a more beautiful setting. Children are sensitive to color and beauty. Young Arizona is growing up with a remarkable background and a great opportunity.

Feeling that her time and energy could be better used, Mary-Russell herself decided about this same time to stop teaching art.

THE SECOND ANNUAL Hopi Craftsman Exhibition was held June 29 to July 6, 1931. Launching the exhibition had required massive effort in 1930, but was somewhat easier in the following years because the proselytizing first visit was no longer necessary and the Coltons could rely on Jimmie or Edmund to return unsold goods and distribute money after the show. The Coltons now needed to go to the reservation three times per year instead of the original five.

The second show was an even bigger success than the first. Sales amounted to $1,300 ($11,349) and Mary-Russell gave $300 ($2,619) in prize money. An added incentive was Mary-Russell's announcement that the managers of an exposition of Indian tribal arts to be held in New York had commissioned her to buy a collection of high-quality goods.

She was able to achieve another of her goals that year when she found a supply of natural indigo in New York. She ordered twenty-five pounds of it on June 13, and began to make it available to the Hopis. As with long staple cotton in 1930, she first offered the indigo to the Indian traders, who did not want to bother with it. So she sold it at cost through the museum, providing much of it to the Hopis by mail order. Later, she was also able to provide the Hopis with cochineal and madder.

BY THIS TIME, eastern art reviewers had begun to look forward to Mary-Russell's Arizona landscapes in the shows of The Ten. In 1931, a Philadelphia newspaper paid her a tribute:

Mary Russell Ferrell Colton takes her artistic joy in the solitary stretches of our southwestern desert lands, from which she culls some marvelously decorative effects. The simplest of all these, Cinder Hills-Hadean Landscape, *is doubtless the most impressive, but one may also take much pleasure in the large and sombre* California Valley *and the deeply vocative* Sunset Crater and Lava Flow. *Her* Hopi Indian Spinner *is a magnificent piece of color.*

Mary-Russell entrusted the details of running the 1931 Exhibition of Arizona Artists Show to Katharine Bartlett and Virgil Hubert, and once it was underway in mid-July, she joined Harold and Ferrell on a vacation trip to Hawaii. The trip also had a scientific aspect, as Harold was in-terested in see-ing the eruption of Mauna Loa, the famous Big Island volcano. The family stayed in Hawaii until the beginning of September, when Ferrell had to return for school.

On September 9, 1931, just after the Coltons returned from Hawaii, Harold's brother Ralph (who had been the architect for Coyote Range) was killed in a freak boat accident. While he was working on the boat's engine, it exploded; Ralph was not injured by the blast itself, but jerked back so vio-lently that his head struck a mortal blow against a door frame. Jessie Colton, the boys' mother, had suffered a slight stoke a few days before Ralph's acci-dent, when Harold was still in Honolulu, and had a relapse when she heard the news about Ralph.

Harold went east for several weeks to take care of family matters, while Mary-Russell and Ferrell stayed in Flagstaff. During Harold's absence, Mary-Russell took over full management of Coyote Range and the activities of the museum, including a dig it was conducting at Wupatki. She also dealt with guests and visitors, a task Harold no doubt enjoyed much more than she. She realized that she was stretching herself too thin and wrote to Harold:

Evidently the time is approaching in my life when I must have a real holiday once in a while, or something, some of the wires might snap. I imagine that the lack of an ovary may make things a bit more difficult too.

In another letter she shed a little light on this comment:

I saw the doctor today & he gave me a hypo of ovarian extract and this after-noon I felt less nervous than I have for some time & the world brightened consid-erably. He said blood pressure & heart were quite OK, so it's only the old nerves again.

In the same letter, she said she hoped Harold could settle everything while he was in Philadelphia,

> *because I do not feel that I should have to make the upsetting trip east this winter, where you know that I am now always very unhappy. The doctor feels that it would be good for me to go to a lower altitude for a little while, where I would have rest without worry.*

Harold, who still had family and friends in the East and enjoyed visiting, made an attempt to go there once a year. Mary-Russell believed in "letting sleeping relatives lie" and preferred to stay home at Coyote Range.

Nonetheless, Mary-Russell accompanied Harold to Philadelphia in November 1931, primarily because she felt she might not have another opportunity to see "Mother Colton" alive. Harold's mother was in the hospital when Harold and Mary-Russell arrived, but was released during their visit and seemed to improve. Mary-Russell had a medical emergency of her own while they were in the Philadelphia area, when her appendix had to be removed.

The Coltons returned to Flagstaff from Philadelphia on February 12, 1932, ready to enter into the whirl of activities that was now their life. In the spring, Mary-Russell devoted time to the Navajo-Hopi boundary dispute, which was then heating up. She wrote letters in behalf of the Hopis, stating her belief that instead of a joint-use area, there should be a definite boundary established, with land staked out that was solely Hopi. She reasoned that if this were not done, the more numerous and more aggressive Navajos would always be able to get the upper hand.

In May, she expressed her thoughts about another federal matter. Officials in the Bureau of Indian Affairs came up with the idea of issuing a government stamp of authenticity, a hallmark complying with federal regulations that would be applied to Indian arts and crafts. She opposed the notion, feeling that the two traders, Pavatea and Hubbell, could control the use of the stamp to funnel all approved goods into their stores. She felt that such a program could inhibit the production of goods for the Hopi Craftsman Exhibition. A modified version of the stamp program was adopted, but it was cumbersome and indifferently enforced, and had little effect on Hopi arts and crafts.

BY THIS TIME, Mary-Russell had developed a calendar for the museum's major shows. First would come the Junior Art Show, in May or June. Next would be the Hopi Craftsman, held around the Fourth of July, the same time as the Pow-Wow celebration that brought thousands of visitors to Flagstaff. The final big event would be the Exhibition of Arizona Artists, in late July or early August. This meant that she was committed to devoting major amounts of time and effort to art exhibitions in the spring and summer, but could relax a bit by mid-August.

In the summer of 1932, Mary-Russell began working on another of the items on her agenda, the improvement of Hopi pottery. From her Hopi friend Poli, she obtained the recipe that Poli's wife Fay used for mixing clay. She then scoured the Painted Desert for colored soils and rocks, looking for natural examples of every color in the palette. She sent samples of these substances to a laboratory in New Jersey to be analyzed so that the mineral providing the color in each specimen could be identified. She also arranged to have a ceramics instructor at the local college conduct scientific firing experiments in a controlled kiln. She compared these results with the results obtained by the traditional firing methods Fay used. Harold helped Mary-Russell with her pottery studies, and their combined knowledge produced significant improvements in the materials and techniques of Hopi pottery.

In the June 1932 issue of *Museum Notes*, Mary-Russell published an article, "Wool for Our Indian Weavers—What Shall It Be?" In it, she discussed her research and recommended that the Indians raise certain traditional strains of sheep in order to meet their needs. Later in the year, she also spoke at two government conferences on wool and textile improvement. Believing that she could not count on the government to do the necessary work, she continued to research and conducted additional experiments on her own.

As part of this research, Mary-Russell corresponded with a sheep breeder in Laramie, Wyoming, J. H. King. On August 11, 1932, she wrote to him that:

> *I deplore the fact that the government has never carried out any scientifically controlled breeding experiments, and has not thoroughly considered the actual requirements of the Indian. I am anxious to carry out a small experiment for demonstration purposes at the Museum.*

From King, she ordered samples of wool from several breeds of sheep. She had these woven into small rugs by Navajo weavers so that the qualities of the various wools could be compared.

ON AUGUST 4, 1932, Harold's mother, weakened by her earlier strokes, died. Harold went east for the funeral, and Mary-Russell and Ferrell stayed home. It was during this time that she began interviewing Edmund Nequatewa, recording his recollections of Hopi legends. This led to an article about Hopi folklore in the October 1932 issue of *Museum Notes*.

In recognition of her academy training as an artist, her experience as a teacher, and her knowledge of Hopi art, she was requested by officials in the Bureau of Indian Affairs to provide ideas about teaching art to students in the Indian schools. In response, she wrote an article about teaching Hopi arts and crafts in the Indian day schools in the fall of 1932, and sent copies to the appropriate officials. One of these, F. H. McBride, principal of the Mishongnovi Day School, wrote her, saying, "Mrs. McBride and I had the pleasure of reading the article. . . . We thought it very excellent. We think it would be a fine thing if our traveling officials could be provided with a copy."

AT THE 1933 meeting of the Board of Trustees of the museum, Mary-Russell was re-elected to the board and appointed curator of ethnology in addition to her existing duties as curator of art. These were not honorary positions; she worked hard at both, particularly the newly assigned task of ethnology. She continued to probe Edmund Nequatewa's knowledge of Hopi folklore, beliefs, and ways. (She eventually became so knowledgeable about the subject that the federal Bureau of Indian Affairs used her as a consultant.)

In April, she successfully staved off a threat to the Hopi Craftsman Exhibition, which—now a success—was attracting imitators. The National Association of Indian Affairs held an annual rodeo in Polacca, and thought that it might expand the event to include an arts and crafts show. This meant that it would be staged about the same time as the Hopi Craftsman Exhibition. Mary-Russell pointed out that there were not enough high-quality goods to support two shows at the same time, and that the effect might be to damage the museum's successful program for no appreciable gain. She suggested that instead, what was really wanted was some sort of show for the Navajos, mentioning that the Hopi Craftsman Exhibition in the previous year had produced some $2,000 ($19,000) dollars for the Hopi artists, plus an additional sixty or seventy orders for custom work. She did not mention—perhaps it was understood—that the money to stage the show and award prizes would have to come from somewhere, and not every arts and crafts exhibition would have a benefactor who was willing to underwrite these expenses as she did in Flagstaff. At any rate, her arguments convinced officials to give up their idea.

The Hopi Craftsman Exhibition continued to grow and improve. Mary-Russell wrote to a friend that

We have just closed our fourth Hopi Show and feel well pleased with the results of the exhibition both financial and artistic. The quality of our material shows a decided advance over least year's work and we can now see that our educational program among the craftsmen is bringing definite results.

PORTRAIT PHOTOGRAPH OF
MARY-RUSSELL, 1934

The Museum of Northern Arizona, under the guidance of the Coltons, was in some respects too successful, for it was desperately short of space. The problem was exacerbated in 1934, when the Monte Vista Hotel directors received an offer from the Isham-Spencer Insurance Agency to rent the storefront that the museum had been using as an annex. A long-range solution to the space problem was necessary, and Mary-Russell came to the rescue. She donated twenty-nine acres of land on the west side of the Fort Valley Road, some three miles north of town, in memory of Sabin. She also rented the Homestead to the

THE FAMILY AT COYOTE RANGE: FERRELL, HAROLD,
MARY-RUSSELL, AND KATHERINE BARTLETT, 1934

museum for a dollar a year. Harold had already sketched plans for a museum building, and he now re-worked these to suit the donated land. Construction of the first buildings began soon afterwards, with funding from Harold.

The Coltons' separately filed income tax returns for the year 1934 give an idea of their capacity for generosity. Harold reported gross income of $47,844 ($475,090), almost all of it interest and dividends from three trusts. He gave charitable contributions of $10,488 ($104,145), mostly to the museum. Mary-Russell's gross income was $2,952 ($29,313). Her contributions included the support of "Elderly retired trained nurse [Bug] and blind colored man [Alex McEuen, an old and disabled servant of the Houston family]." Their combined gross income was $50,796 ($504,404).

MARY-RUSSELL'S EFFORTS in making long staple cotton available to the Hopis were successful, and led to the following statement to the *Coconino Sun* during the 1934 Hopi Craftsman Exhibition:

Since long staple cotton has been procured by the museum for the Hopi, beautiful handspun cotton wedding robes and fringed belts may again be seen, like those made in the ancient days when the Hopi grew their own peculiar type of cotton.

The article about art education that Mary-Russell wrote and circulated in 1933 was such a hit that she expanded it and published it in book form as a museum bulletin entitled, *Art for the Schools of the Southwest: An Outline for the Public and Indian Schools,* in 1934. It was given wide circulation.

Writing the book gave her a new awareness of the art education situation in northern Arizona. Few teachers had any training in art, and many of the schools were located far from art exhibitions. To provide some assistance, Mary-Russell created what she called the "Treasure Chest." She had a pirate chest built and stuffed it with art materials and teaching guides, then sent it on rounds of the public schools, paying for it out of her own purse. The chest contained objects intended to delight children, to foster an appreciation of beautiful things, and to impress upon them that they were themselves capable of creating beautiful and useful objects. It was so well received and widely admired that Mary-Russell had another one built and equipped for the Indian schools.

Mary-Russell had firm ideas about teaching arts and crafts to Indian children. The federal government was at that time (and had been for many years) engaged in the practice of "assimilation," trying in every respect to make Indian children shed their native beliefs and become members of the mainstream culture. Consistent with this practice, children were being taught European-inspired art. Mary-Russell believed this to be a mistake, saying "All Indian teachers should have a background course in the history and customs of the people with whom they are to work." She advocated for the federal government's development of standards for teaching Indian children. Ideally, these would require teachers to have sound training in arts and crafts and to teach the children the arts of their individual tribe. Overall, she suggested that everything be rooted in the environment.

IN HER NEVER-ENDING quest to help Hopis, she and Harold became involved in an effort in 1934 that on paper seemed like a good idea but in practice was a comic-opera exercise in government red tape and inefficiency. The Coltons learned that park rangers planned to thin the buffalo herd at Yellowstone and would make available to Indian tribes buffalo meat, hooves, and horns. Thinking that this might be a boon to the Hopis, Mary-Russell arranged to acquire some of the buffalo.

Apparently the buffalo program was one of those "first step" ideas, one in which someone has a good idea (the first step), but that no one really thinks through. It is a long way from Yellowstone, Montana, to Keams Canyon, Arizona, and transporting fifteen perishable buffalo carcasses between the two points in good condition was no easy task. After a summer of frustration, the buffalo parts were dropped of at the railroad depot at Holbrook, Arizona. The Coltons then had to hire a school bus to transport the cargo sixty miles to Keams Canyon. Harold, Mary-Russell, and Katharine Bartlett then drove around the Hopi towns, distributing the buffalo parts. Never again did the Coltons try to render assistance to the Hopis via the buffalo control program.

While Mary-Russell was on the Hopi reservation that fall, however, she and Harold noticed—as they had previously—that many of the babies were ill with a disease called "the summer complaint," which was sometimes fatal. They observed that Hopi children frequently drank from small pools that contained dirty, possibly contaminated water. Mary-Russell wrote to the field nurse at the Indian Hospital in Toreva, suggesting that drinking this dirty water might be a cause of the disease. There is no record that anything ever came of this, but the incident illustrates the many ways in which she sought to help her Hopi friends.

THROUGHOUT THE THIRTIES, Mary-Russell acted as a judge at various art shows, both Indian and non-Indian. She continued to participate in the annual exhibitions of The Ten and held a few exhibitions of her work in Flagstaff, at the museum and the local college. As an expert in Indian art, she also fielded many inquiries, some for information; others were from people who wanted to buy genuine high-quality Indian goods. She took upon herself the task of acting as a broker, putting buyers in touch with Hopi artists, always donating her time.

By 1935, during the depths of the Depression, economizing was on everyone's mind, and public institutions in particular were seeking ways to reduce expenditures. In a pattern common across the country, the Flagstaff School Board decided that one way to save money was to cut unnecessary subjects from the school curriculum. The board announced that art was nonessential and targeted it as the first program to be eliminated.

This provoked Mary-Russell to write a strong appeal, published in the May 1935 issue of *Museum Notes*. She titled the article, "The Museum Asks Help for the Children of Arizona," and stated her belief that "art education is both a practical and liberal education in life and is closely and inextricably correlated with every other subject in the school." In spite of her plea, however, the schools cut art.

Soon after, the Coltons began the second phase of the building program on the land Mary-Russell donated in 1934, with the construction of four more units. One of the benefits of having the museum located near Coyote Range was that Mary-Russell could now walk to it.

In the fall of 1935, Harold and Ferrell went to Philadelphia, where they visited relatives and friends and Harold attended a science conference. Mary-Russell stayed home. Harold appreciated and valued Mary-Russell but apparently neglected to tell her so, though she longed to hear it. As so often happens, it took an intermediary to carry the message. Ferrell wrote to Mary-Russell on November 18 from Philadelphia:

I no longer have the slightest doubt of what Dad thinks of you and your abilities, for all I have heard since coming on this trip is continual talk of you, your doings and your abilities. I am now fully convinced that you are the most competent person that has been seen for a long time. Why, the man stands around and boasts of the things you do and the way you do them. Why, lady, you have a husband that does nothing but talk of art projects, farming, treasure chests, Indian crafts, etc. I sometimes have difficulty in believing my ears.

ON FEBRUARY 29, 1936, the location in the Woman's Club was closed and the museum moved to the new exhibit hall on the land that Mary-Russell had donated. It took a while, however, for everything to be moved into the new quarters and made ready for the public.

Early in April 1936, the Southwest Division of the American Association for the Advancement of Science held its annual conference in Flagstaff. Mary-Russell hosted a tea for the attendees at Coyote Range and then took the visitors on a tour of the new museum exhibits building, which was almost finished. The public opening of the new exhibit hall occurred soon afterward, on May 2, following a private showing for members and donors on April 25. This was a major event in the lives of the Coltons and the life of the museum; Mary-Russell acted as hostess at both openings.

Occupied by moving everything into the new building, Mary-Russell decided not to hold the Arizona Artists Show in 1936, which would have been its eighth year. Although she spoke of a temporary cancellation in her comments to the Board of Trustees, the Exhibition of Arizona Artists was never revived. With this cancellation, her roster of annual shows was reduced to two, the Junior Art Show in May and the Hopi Craftsman Exhibition in July.

In 1936 she turned her attention to helping Navajo art through the organization of a Navajo Arts and Crafts Exhibition. Held at Wupatki, it was a small show but a step in the right direction and was the impetus for the full-blown Navajo shows that were later sponsored by the museum. Mary-Russell donated the prize money in the name of the museum. She and her Navajo friend Peshlakai Etcitty (also spelled Etcidy) were the judges.

FERRELL, WHO BY now was following a career as a merchant seaman, suggested an around-the-world trip to his parents in 1936. Although she generally preferred to stay close to home, Mary-Russell entered enthusiastically into the ambitious travel project. After much planning and preparation, she temporarily resigned as curator of art and ethnology and turned the duties over to Virgil Hubert. Then, on December 10, Harold and Mary-Russell embarked on their journey, traveling up the West Coast by train to Seattle, where they were joined by Ferrell. The three then went to Vancouver and sailed for Hawaii on December 12.

Mary-Russell took art materials along and also kept a journal. The entries are alive with color and vivid impressions. The first is particularly poignant:

I am going around the world! We three, my husband, my son and I. We have had many happy journeys together, we enjoy each other's company. I am forty-seven years old and have always dreamed of traveling in the East— Japan, China, India. It is true my fathers stories may come true and I will really see the places turn into reality from the stories told me by him so long ago.

From Hawaii, they went to Japan, then landed in Shanghai. Her last entry for 1936 described a temple they visited while in China:

The dark interior of a large temple, the snake of incense rising to the dim golden figure of Gautama Buddha flanked by two lesser figures of Wisdom and Mercy and surrounded by the minor figures of the disciples against the blackened walls. At a table a priest is dispensing remedies to the poor, the sufferer draws forth a small stick from a jar, the priest reads the number on it, looks up this number in his book of remedies and prescribes for the patient. As we pass through the temple we see a small white clothed figure standing in the dark, a pile of tinsel [silver] paper of temple money at his feet and joss sticks smoking on the floor. This little lad is in mourning and offering homage to the dead.

On New Year's Day 1937, the Coltons arrived in Hong Kong. They visited only briefly before sailing to Manila, which they reached on January 3. After some sightseeing in the city, they went into the hinterlands; a few days later, as they were being driven on a dangerous jungle road in the back country, Mary-Russell became quite apprehensive. "Of course, when an old time Arizonian has a creepy feeling in the pit of his tummy on account of the condition of a road, it really means something." It is telling to note that Mary-Russell no longer regarded herself as a Philadelphian or an Easterner, but as an Arizonian—a profound change that had taken place within the span of ten years.

By January 25, they were sailing again and nearing the Equator:

Peeped out at dawn. Beautiful dark blue land, quite near, mountains in silhouette against a sky like a fire opal, purple clouds against a fiery rose red and gold, reflections in a glassy sea.

ON THEIR AROUND-THE-WORLD TRIP, IN THE PHILIPPINES.
MARY-RUSSELL SKETCHES WHILE HAROLD TAKES A NAP, 1937

Near the end of January, they landed in Bali, and were so busy that Mary-Russell just entered a few words for each day at the top of the daily pages with the remainder of the page blank, as if intending to fill it in later. While they were there, they visited anthropologist Margaret Meade and her husband Gregory Bateson, who lived on the island.

They left Bali on February 10, sailing by Sourabaja, Djocja, and Batavia (Jakarta). On February 17, they landed at Singapore and spent some time there. It was not until February 23, when they were at sea once more, that Mary-Russell began entering full descriptions again, recording their experiences in Burma and India.

By the beginning of March, they were in the foothills of the Himalayas; they arose early to see the sunrise on Mt. Everest:

As we hurried down the trail to our car, the Butian rickshaw boys passed merrily trotting down with their loaded chairs and rickshaws. They sang as they went and how strange, it might have been our Navajo singing in the dawn.

Her writing stopped completely with an entry made in Bombay on March 16. By this time she had been traveling for three months, and was exhausted.

From India, the Coltons sailed to Egypt, where they took in the usual tourist sights, and ended their stay in Alexandria. They sailed through the Suez Canal, then stopped in Greece and Italy, so Harold could revisit the *Zoologica Stazione*, near Naples, where he spent several months as a post-graduate student in 1909.

Leaving Italy, they visited Sicily and Algeria, then sailed through the Straits of Gibraltar, stopping at Lisbon and the Azores on the route home. When they reached New York, they parted company with Ferrell and boarded the train to Flagstaff. Their grand trip was over. They had traveled on eleven ocean liners and twenty-four different railroad trains, visited fifteen countries, and handled twelve different kinds of currency. Of all the places they had visited, Mary-Russell's favorite was Bali.

By this time, Mary-Russell was clearly ill, and as the train headed west, her condition worsened. A doctor examined her in Chicago and said she had a cold. By the time they reached Lamy, New Mexico, she knew she had something worse. Mary-Russell and Harold left the train and went to Santa Fe, where a doctor diagnosed her illness as scarlet fever and hospitalized her for a day. The Coltons finally returned to Flagstaff in mid-May 1937.

Once at home and recuperated, Mary-Russell resumed her busy schedule of farming, painting, hosting exhibitions at the museum, and advancing the interests of art. Re-appointed curator of art and ethnology at the annual director's meeting of the museum June 4, she hosted the ninth Hopi Craftsman Exhibition and attended the Snake Dance at Shungopavi. She was also able to spend hours in her studio, turning her portfolio of sketches from the trip into finished paintings.

By now, Mary-Russell realized that she would never have the time to do the intensive study of Hopi botany that she desired, so she and Harold hired a student from the University of Michigan, Alfred F. Whiting, to live with the Hopis and conduct field studies. His work resulted in a book, *Ethnobotany of the Hopi*, published in 1939. It became the standard in the field and is still considered an authoritative work.

IN 1938, THE City of Flagstaff was having trouble meeting its expenses and felt it necessary to cut many programs. One of the targets was the public library. Mary-Russell made donations to help save the library, which—with her help and the help of others—survived. Gertrude Hill, who became the librarian, wrote to Mary-Russell and described her first view of the library:

> *The excellent files of well-mounted and carefully classified illustrations of all sorts which you so thoughtfully provided for the use of the local school teachers and their pupils, the innumerable gifts of fine books and periodicals to augment the Library's collections, your many personal courtesies and helpful suggestions in connection with our work, are all bright spots in my memory.*

One of Mary-Russell's best ideas, the Hopi Silver Project, was conceived in 1938. When she had first formulated her plans for improving Indian art after her move to Flagstaff, she decided to address first the ailing arts of pottery and textiles. Acting on her plan, she devoted most of her efforts in the early years of the Hopi Craftsman Exhibition to the improvement of these crafts. The plan worked, and pottery and weaving became robust. The next art to receive her attention was basketry, and by 1938, it, too, was in much healthier condition. The sick man of Hopi arts was silver work.

Mary-Russell, with the help of her Hopi employees, conducted a survey and found that there were only twelve Hopi silversmiths living on the reservation. These smiths worked part time at their craft and each sold about twenty-five dollars worth of jewelry each year. Practically their only market was the Hopi Craftsman Exhibition.

The federal government, which had an erratic record in its efforts to assist Indian arts and crafts, had created an Indian Arts and Crafts Board in 1935. Soon after its creation, the board adopted a cumbersome method of awarding federal hallmarks to Indian artisans who met certain standards. If a piece of jewelry was produced in compliance with the requirements, the artist had to contact a federal agent, who would send an inspector living nearby to view the work. If the inspector was satisfied that all the rules had been followed, he would issue a certificate allowing the government stamp of authenticity to be placed on the piece. Mary-Russell realized that this concern for authenticity addressed the problem of machine-made imitation jewelry but missed the main point, which was that Hopi silver was itself an imitation art.

As she wrote,

> (1) [Hopi silver] is practically without character, just more poor "Navajo"
> (2) it is quite what one would expect of an art frankly copied from another
> people (3) in very rare instances has it occurred to the Hopi smith to use
> Hopi design.

Mary-Russell's inspiration was to apply authentic Hopi designs, symbols, and motifs to silverwork, using some of the figures that worked so well and were so distinctive on Hopi basketry, pottery, and textiles. She discussed her idea with Harold and Virgil Hubert, the museum's assistant art director. Hubert took the task in hand and worked on ideas. He had two breakthroughs: transferring Hopi symbols from pottery and basketry to jewelry, and using the overlay technique. He sketched and painted fifteen suggested pieces of silverwork using authentic Hopi symbols.

Once Hubert had made his sketches and his invaluable suggestion to use the overlay process, he dropped out of the picture, and the rest of the work on the Hopi Silver Project was done by Mary-Russell. On November 14, 1938, she wrote a first batch of letters to all of the known Hopi silversmiths, on and off the reservation. With each letter she sent a photograph of a piece of the proposed Virgil Hubert jewelry, offering to buy the jewelry if the smith would produce it according to the picture. She also proposed that pieces of the new jewelry be entered in the 1939 Hopi Craftsman Exhibition.

She felt obliged to follow the government hallmark program as well, so the offer to the Hopi smiths was two-pronged: the new silver must comply with the hallmark standards and must look like the Hubert designs.

A large portion of Mary-Russell's time and attention in 1939 was devoted to the Hopi Silver project. She wrote many letters soliciting participation, and dealt with responses. Of the eighteen smiths contacted, some made no reply, a few indicated they were hostile to the idea, and seven sent jewelry to her. The pieces submitted by three of the seven were rejected as unacceptable— crudely made and not in accordance to the plan.

In spite of all of her efforts, by the time of the 1939 Hopi Craftsman

Exhibition, the results were meager. Four artists had crafted a dozen acceptable pieces of jewelry. She displayed these and awaited public reaction. The worth of her idea was quickly proven, as the pieces of the new overlay jewelry were an instant hit. All the jewelry was sold and orders were placed for more. The new style was attractive and distinctive, no longer a pale imitation of Navajo work. It clearly identified itself as something new, different, and beautiful. Mary-Russell continued to encourage the Hopi Silver Project, and worked to enlist more artists to participate.

SHE WAS STILL painting, though her dwindling vigor and multiple duties made it difficult. As Mary-Russell wrote to her friend and art school classmate, Isabel Cartwright, "I am working hard in the studio every day now and believe I am going to be able to come out even. It seems very hard to get uninterrupted time which is so important to really accomplish anything."

Mary-Russell traveled east for the last time in her life in the fall of 1939, when she and Harold visited Ferrell on his merchant ship at South Portland, Maine. Thereafter, Harold attended the meeting of the American Philosophical Society in Philadelphia and presented a paper, while Mary-Russell visited friends and caught up with happenings in the art world. She also visited her widowed aunt, Lucia Hull, whom she found living in a dingy apartment in New York with little support. Ever generous, she began supporting Mrs. Hull, for whose care she paid $1,600 ($15,312) annually.

Chapter Six

MATURITY

BY 1940, MARY-RUSSELL had turned fifty, her health was beginning to fail, and her many duties were becoming burdensome. After conducting the Hopi Craftsman Exhibition for eleven years, she decided to get some help in staging the show. Harold wrote Isabelle Kelly, extending a job offer to her in March:

> *Mrs. Colton has not been very well and her doctor wants her to give up her work with the Hopis during the summer. We do not want to drop that work and the rest of our staff are busy with their own duties. We are wondering if you would be interested in taking on this job for the summer. . . .*

Though Mary-Russell's health and energy were failing, she was nonetheless driven to pursue her mission. She staged the Hopi Craftsman Exhibition in 1940, where more of the Hopi Silver Project jewelry was submitted, and it became clear that silversmith Paul Saufkie of Shungopavi was going to be its leading practitioner and exponent. He appeared as a demonstrator, making some of the jewelry in view of the patrons. He sold all of his pieces and took home orders for a dozen more. The museum was by this time conducting a lively mail-order business for Hopi arts and crafts, overseen by Mary-Russell.

As far as her own art was concerned, 1940 was the last year she would enter paintings in the exhibitions of The Ten. She sent in three works, all of which had been painted and exhibited previously: *Autumn Glow, Arizona; Dressing for the Dance, Bali;* and *Dawn Glow, Arizona.*

In March 1941, Mary-Russell lost the woman who had been her closest friend in Flagstaff, Mary Morton Pollock, who died while staying in Pasadena with her sister. Friends had no doubt that Mrs. Pollock died of a broken heart caused by the death of her husband, T. E. Pollock, in 1938.

In 1941, Mary-Russell followed through on an idea she had ten years earlier, which was to build a museum gift shop for the Hopis on the reservation. With the aid of Edmund Nequatewa, the Coltons located a suitable site outside the village of Shungopavi. Harold drew plans for a building and the Coltons paid to have stones collected and piled up nearby in the fall, hoping to construct the building in the summer of 1942. (World War II prevented the construction. It was not until 1968 that the Hopis built a Cultural Center on the site.)

Then Mary-Russell and Harold spent six weeks at Laguna Beach, California, hoping that a vacation and lower altitude would benefit her health. On December 7, 1941, an event that shook the world changed the lives of the Coltons and everyone they knew. Harold described how they learned of it:

When Mary-Russell, Katharine Bartlett and I returned home from a trip to the Big Sandy and Walapai Mt., on December 7, 1941, we heard over the radio the announcement of the attack on Pearl Harbor.

The despair she felt manifested itself in a variety of ways. As Harold noted:

When World War II began in 1941, she lost all interest in painting. She could see no point in art work and gave her attention to the Red Cross, organizing and administering a nurse's aid[e] course in the Flagstaff Community Hospital.

All of her life, she had worn her hair long, reaching below her waist. During the war years, she made her one-and-only visit to a beauty parlor and had her hair cut short. After the war ended, she let it grow long again. Ferrell's enlistment in the Coast Guard on December 8, the day after the bombing, was no doubt another source of worry to her. Basic training waived due to his seafaring experience, he was immediately stationed at Port Hueneme, California.

For some time Mary-Russell had hoped that Ferrell would get married and start a family. During his stay in California, he met Dortha Heck Tollhurst, who was on the brink of a divorce. On March 23, 1942, Ferrell and Dortha were married in Oxnard, California, in a small ceremony attended by the bride's parents and Harold and Mary-Russell.

Back in Flagstaff, Harold accepted appointment as the director of the American Red Cross for the Flagstaff area, and in mid-April 1942, Mary-Russell agreed to assist by acting as the chair of the Red Cross's Nurse's Aide program.

The war had an immediate impact on this northern Arizona community. Many residents went into military service and war work, including museum employees. Rationing of critical materials such as gasoline and rubber began. Mary-Russell had to make changes in the museum's art program. Schools were unable to attend the Junior Art Show, so she canceled the 1942 exhibition, which would have been the twelfth in the series. She was, however, able to present eight other shows. One of these was the museum's first Navajo Craftsman Exhibition. The Hopi Craftsman Exhibition was also held, and Mary-Russell was pleased to see that the Hopi silver she had launched in 1938 appeared in greater quantities and was eagerly purchased by the public. These 1942 shows were to be the last until after the war; wartime conditions forced her to suspend them for the duration.

The war caused other disruptions, as the hand of government reached ever farther into civilian life. The War Production Board decided that wool was a strategic material, and passed a regulation forbidding its use for non-essential purposes, such as making rugs. Bureaucrats had Georgia carpet mills in mind, and were ignorant of the devastating effect the regulation would have on Indian weavers who depended on the sale of hand-woven textiles for their livelihood. Mary-Russell wrote federal officials about the problem, asking for relief for the Hopis and Navajos, and an exemption was created in their favor. Soon afterward, the same thing happened to silver, and again, she helped them get relief.

As the war overshadowed all civilian endeavors, Mary-Russell had one final inspiration concerning Hopi silver. She could see that it had the potential to become the most vital Hopi art of all and that it would be wise to provide the best possible conditions to make and market it. With this in mind, she suggested that the Hopis form a guild of silversmiths. She wrote the Bureau of Indian Affairs in Window Rock for information about the Navajo Guild, thinking that it could perhaps serve as a model. She also wrote to influential Hopi artist Fred Kabotie, saying,

> It has always been my hope . . . that a shop for the sale of Hopi Arts and Crafts and for the placement of orders, could be established on the Reservation. If you come to Flagstaff at any time, please come to see me. I will always be interested in the Hopi and their work and I am glad to do what I can to help.

But for the intervention of the war, Mary-Russell's efforts might very well have resulted in the formation of a Hopi guild in 1942.

The war-created labor shortage made it impossible for the Coltons to find household servants, so Mary-Russell began to run the house by herself. Her routine was described by Katharine Bartlett: Harold was usually the first to rise in the morning and fixed a cup of coffee. While he was drinking it, Mary-Russell got up and prepared the breakfast. Harold went to his office while Mary-Russell took care of the dishes and planned the meals for the day. The biggest meal was eaten at lunch time. Katharine was usually responsible for the lighter evening meal, after which Harold would take part in dishwashing. If Mary-Russell needed to go to town, Harold or Katharine drove her.

Mary-Russell contributed to the war effort by writing a summary of her work on Hopi dyes at the request of army officials, who thought the knowledge might help troops in the field find camouflage materials. She also experimented with making varnish from the gum of the piñon pine.

But her primary war work was acting as chair of the Nurse's Aide program. Her first graduating class of fifteen women received their caps in a ceremony hosted by the Coltons at the Monte Vista Hotel on December 18, 1942. This class was followed by others. Mary-Russell thought that her Nurse's Aide effort was worthwhile, believing that it brought about many improvements in the "terrible hospital situation" in Flagstaff. She also donated an ambulance to the program.

In January 1943, Mary-Russell published her first work since 1939, an article entitled "An Appreciation of the Art of Nampeyo and Her Influence

have done such good work for the museum, that I find it impossible to act as a judge between you.

The time has come when I feel that you should look around for some position that will suit you better and where you can have more space for your large and increasing family. I advise you while you are on the reservation, to see if there is not some place in the Indian Service where your specialized training can be used, where the work would be of a kind that you would like, and the pay adequate. I will be glad to give you any help that I can and would like to see you in a comfortable position before severing your connection with the museum.

Therefore I am writing you now as a friend & giving you the best advice that I can. I sincerely believe that at this time when help is so hard to get would be an excellent time for you to look for a position.

When I know the date when I will return home I will advise you. In the meantime, in order to earn your pay from the museum, I wish you (1) to collect any stories bearing on Hopi History that you can from old men and write them down and (2) record for me any sites with pottery with Deadman Black on white, Kana-a- Black on white or Lino Black on Gray. Collect a sack of sherds and make a map showing the position of the sites. For it to be any good, I must know the exact location. Do not bother with a letter.

Edmund left his employment at the museum on November 1, 1944. Even so, he remained on good terms with the Coltons, naming one of his sons Harold and one of his daughters Mary-Russell.

As the year drew to a close, there was also a new beginning. After her stay with Mary-Russell and Harold, Dortha had moved to Los Angeles to live with her parents while Ferrell was overseas. On December 15, 1944, Dortha Colton presented Mary-Russell with another granddaughter, Ferrell Denise Colton, born in Los Angeles.

AT THE ANNUAL meeting of the trustees of the museum in February 1945, Mary-Russell declared her intention to make her third major land donation, part of the former farm land and its buildings, in memory of Sabin. The gift of the farm property was of great value. Located across from the exhibits building on the east side of Fort Valley Road, it was a natural site for a campus. The property, which included a dairy barn, three chicken houses, two implement sheds, a potato cellar, and other buildings, was slated to be used as a research facility.

THE FINAL SHOW of The Ten was held in 1945. Its annual exhibitions had been presented continuously since 1917, when the group was organized. Mary-Russell was one of the founding members and had dutifully sent in works—with few exceptions—from 1917 through 1940, after which she no longer participated. During the life of the organization, thirty members came and went, but three belonged for the entire period: Isabel Cartwright, Constance Cochrane, and Mary-Russell.

ON MAY 8, 1945 (VE-Day), Germany surrendered, followed on August 15 by VJ-Day, when hostilities with Japan ended. The servicemen began returning. Corky Jones left the Colton home to reunite with her husband, but many others came back to the museum, and new members were added to the staff. The organization began to rebuild. Virgil Hubert, who returned in July 1945, undertook as one of his first tasks assisting Mary-Russell in staging an exhibition called "The Arts and Crafts of Bali and Java." Through this show, she was able to share with the public some of the beloved objects she had acquired in her earlier "round-the-world" trip.

Mary-Russell assumed that the end of the war meant that her life would return to its pre-war condition, but she found that there had been many losses in the interim. She had lost the urge to paint. The dissolution of The Ten removed her incentive, and the shock of the war still disturbed her, the thought that so much could be destroyed so senselessly. For the first time since 1913, she began to list her occupation on her income tax return as "housewife" rather than "artist." She was no longer farming. The most significant difference, however, was in her health. She did not have the vigor required to do all that she had undertaken. She resigned as the museum's curator of art in 1946 and took a much less active position as chairman of the art committee.

Her health became a constant problem, a matter of increasing concern for herself and Harold. Although not particularly old—she was fifty-seven in March 1946—she began to experience problems associated with aging.

During the war, the Coltons had not gone to a warmer climate at a lower elevation during the winters as had been their custom. Now, hoping that a winter in a warmer climate might improve her "nervous condition," the Coltons and Katharine Bartlett spent the winter of 1946 in Santa Barbara. Ferrell was living there, as was Bug, thanks to Mary-Russell's generosity.

While she was in Santa Barbara Mary-Russell had a thorough examination in a clinic, where she was seen by a number of specialists and was given a battery of tests. The report from the clinic described Mary-Russell's general condition:

> *You complained of changes in your nervous system, sinus infection, frontal headaches, burning of your tongue and exhaustion. You stated that you had been working very hard on a ranch in Arizona and that you had had responsibilities of a museum in that area. You believed that there were many factors in making you extremely "nervous." You felt that all of your "nerve endings" were hypersensitive.*
>
> *[Your mother was of] a nervous type. . . .*
>
> *Weight:*
>
> *Best: 138 Lbs.*
>
> *Average: 120 Lbs.*
>
> *Present 120 Lbs.*
>
> *General Appearance: Small, wiry, rather tense woman of 57 years of age. Does not appear chronically ill.*
>
> *The chief features that must be considered in your examination are related to your nervous system. Environmental problems during the war, over work as well as some frustrations regarding your avocation in painting are believed to be major factors in producing your tension.*

The recommendation of the clinic doctors was to address the nervous tension with sedatives and to treat her delayed menopause with hormones.

The winter in Santa Barbara turned out to be an unsuccessful experiment. Harold wrote that "As none of us were very happy at Santa Barbara, we were away from the tools of our work, and I could see no improvement in Mary-Russell's nerves, we decided not to make any permanent commitments." They returned to Flagstaff. Mary-Russell wrote the doctors in Santa Barbara on

June 1, 1947:

Since my return, you will be glad to know, that I have been feeling better, but
under any kind of strain I do not hold up very well. . . .

The hormone tablets began to affect me so violently several weeks ago, that I
reduced the dose to one tablet a week but they still make me miserable for about
four days after each dose. Shall I stop?

At times I feel intensely nervous and I feel that I must take something.

In spite of her condition, Mary-Russell continued to help others. The
Navajos needed and got her help in 1947, when a bill was introduced in Congress to reduce the federal allocation to the Navajos by one-third. The
Navajos appealed to their friends for help, and the Coltons heeded the call,
working with others to stave off the reduction. One of their allies in the fight
was Philip Johnston, the man who created the Navajo Code Talker program
during the war. They were able to prevent the cut.

In 1947, Mary-Russell decided that the museum was able to revive two of
her favorites, the Junior Art Show and the Hopi Craftsman Exhibition. She
was apprehensive about the Hopi show: could it survive a five-year absence?
Would the public remember? Mary-Russell made one trip to the reservation
for this exhibition, with the balance of the collecting work done by museum
employees and Fred Kabotie. She also served as a judge. The show opened on
July 4, at the same time as the Pow-Wow. Demonstrators, including Paul
Saufkie, came in from the reservation to perform their arts for the public. Her
fears were put to rest. She had built well—a recordbreaking crowd of 2,400
people attended the first post-war Hopi Craftsman Exhibition.

Activities at the museum were booming, as it constantly expanded programs, facilities, and staff. While this burst of activity was healthy for the
museum, it was hard on Mary-Russell. Gone were the days when she knew
everyone and could drop in on them daily, chat about what was happening,
and serve a cozy tea at four o'clock. Harold continued to be a strong presence
in the operation of the museum, but Mary-Russell became an outsider.

She began to turn into a recluse. Always shy, she had previously forced herself to appear in public for the good of the causes she served. Now, with her official duties curtailed and her health becoming a consuming concern, she cloistered herself at Coyote Range. When she had to appear for occasions, such as the judging at the Hopi Craftsman Exhibition, she could put on a good face, participating in the event and hiding her problems from the public. But she stopped going to conferences with Harold, and before long, insisted that he stay home with her. She was still able-bodied but her mind was failing.

During these years, Ferrell was living in Santa Barbara, where he was involved in a variety of businesses. Things were not going well for him and he confided this to his parents. They wrote him a jointly composed letter in 1947, stating "It is now clear to us that we all have arrived at a kind of cross-roads in our lives, and it is time that we view with absolute realism our future progress."

Harold went on to sum up his and Mary-Russell's lives:

[O]n founding the museum, your mother and I have created an academic atmosphere in which the stereotype standards of a university are absent, so that one can enter it without specific preparation if he has the desire to do creative work.

This atmosphere is congenial to your mother and to me and has long since become our life. Here we meet interesting people, scientific and artistic, people like ourselves, busy and creative, with intellectual interests. We have friends who visit us from round the globe.

You must see, my son, that we can never leave our home and our work! It is best for you to understand that we cannot be happy without it, nor would we live long deprived of that which we have created for the benefit of others, and in so doing, have found happiness.

Here in Arizona everyone knows us and we are respected; it is not lonely, we and our state belong together, we helped to build it. In Arizona the name of Colton means something.

You could carry forward this work if you would, most ably, there is no one else to do this.

Harold and Mary-Russell invited Ferrell to return to Flagstaff and work for the museum, with the understanding that he was apprenticing to take over when they were no longer able to manage it. Harold added a valuable induce-ment:

> *My father gave us a house as a wedding present, that is what I have always wished to do for you and your family. We will build you a home somewhat larger than your present residence, costing approximately $20,000 [$119,000].*

Ferrell wanted to stay near the ocean and ships. Dortha wanted the secu-rity of a salaried job. The pressure applied by her, Harold, and Mary-Russell finally persuaded Ferrell to return to Flagstaff.

Although her health and energy were fading, Mary-Russell stayed as busy as possible, trying to carry out her life's mission. As she wrote to Fred Kabotie in January 1948:

> *I am beginning to plan for next summer and especially for the Hopi Craftsman Exhibition. As you know, the affairs of the Hopi continue to concern me deeply and it has worried me not to be able to do personally so many of the things that I used to do.*
>
> *As you and Alice have probably guessed, I have not been in the best of health for a year or so, and Doctor and I are not growing any younger. This means that we must save our strength for the many responsibilities that we must meet. Although we both expect to come to the villages in the spring, we did not feel able to make our usual fall trip, when, of course, it was always our habit, before the war, to visit everyone and talk with them about the work for the next summer's exhibition. This, of course, was especially important in the case of the weavers who do most of their weaving in the winter season.*

Another of Mary-Russell's links to the museum was broken in October 1948 when Virgil Hubert left, seeking higher pay. An employee since 1931, he had worked closely with Mary-Russell. They knew each other well and she could rely on Hubert to understand and carry out her wishes. His replacement was an untested New Yorker, Leon Bushman. Appointed curator of art on December 10, 1948, he tendered his resignation on July 27, 1949. Among the reasons he cited for leaving was that he "lacked the confidence of the Chairman of Art [Mary-Russell]." He was replaced by A. O. Brodie, who worked out well and got along with everyone.

In December 1948, Ferrell moved to Flagstaff with his wife Dortha and their daughters, Robin and Denise. Mary-Russell gave Ferrell four acres of land adjacent to Coyote Range and he built a home on it, christening it "Longridge." Ferrell went to work for the museum as secretary-treasurer. Mary-Russell was pleased to have her granddaughters living nearby and enjoyed visiting with them.

Mary-Russell was scheduled to give a presentation at the Heard Museum in Phoenix that month. Although she described herself as a "timid speaker" she had always kept her speaking engagements. Not this time, however. She backed out at the last minute, and Harold had to fill in for her. This was a radical change from her former behavior, as she had always been duty- and honor bound, one who could be counted on to keep her commitments.

THE 1949 HOPI Craftsman Exhibition was one of the crowning moments in Mary-Russell's campaign to rescue Hopi art, proving conclusively the worth of her Hopi Silver Project.

The press alerted the public that a number of Hopi veterans were attending a jewelry-making school taught by Fred Kabotie and Paul Saufkie, and their works would be on display for the first time. People attended in great numbers, eager to find out about the new silver. What they found was a dazzling array. Visitors snapped up the jewelry eagerly and the smiths were deluged with orders for more. It was a triumph, and no one missed the significance of the event. Mary-Russell's ideas had launched a new era. It was one of her proudest moments. Fred Kabotie acknowledged the debt of the Hopis in 1965:

> I want to say in behalf of the Hopi Tribe, that the Hopi indebtedness to Dr. and Mrs. Harold S. Colton is beyond our expression of gratitude. We are indebted for their deep interest and effort in the survival and keeping alive the indigenous Hopi arts and crafts for the appreciation on the part of the general public and for the benefit of the Hopi people. The idea and the inspiration of the Hopi over lay jewelry had been evolved through their foresight.

Due to the success of the new silverwork, the Hopis needed more of an outlet than even the Hopi Craftsman Exhibition could provide, some means of providing constant market access to their work. After reviewing their options, they acted upon the suggestion that Mary-Russell had made in 1942: a group of six of the veterans' school's graduates, together with their tutors, Fred Kabotie and Paul Saufkie, created the Hopi Silver Craft Cooperative Guild. The Hopis kept in touch with Mary-Russell about their progress, and sent her a copy of the Articles of Incorporation of the Hopi Silver Craft Cooperative Guild for review.

ALTHOUGH THE COLTONS had not found Santa Barbara to their liking, the idea of having a winter home at lower altitude was still appealing. They searched for a likely place, and in 1949, finally settled on seven-and-a-half acres in a new subdivision called Color Cove, just west of Sedona. This location had the advantage of being some 2,500 feet lower than Flagstaff, yet only forty miles distant. They hoped that the change would stimulate a change for the better in Mary-Russell; the hope was in vain.

Chapter Seven

DECLINE

WHILE THE 1930S had been a fertile period of extraordinary creativity, a decade when Mary-Russell rose to the heights of her talent and was extremely productive, the 1940s were punctuated by the disruptions of war and the onset of serious emotional distress. In the 1950s, this illness began to dominate her life. Ferrell recalled later that, "Mother's increasing atherosclerosis of the brain began to have a very negative effect on her life and work about 1950." While her doctors diagnosed her condition as "atherosclerosis of the brain," a modern diagnosis would likely have been Alzheimer's disease.

The illness was insidious, and began to affect all areas of her life and the lives of those about her. On the surface, it often appeared that she was her old self, but inside, disturbing changes were occurring. One of the most unsettling things about her condition was that the symptoms manifested as personality changes, in many instances turning her into the opposite of what she had been. Better understood today, Alzheimer's disease in the 1950s was mistaken for nothing more than an alteration of character due to advancing age. People thought that Mary-Russell was simply becoming cranky and eccentric. The family did not understand what was happening, and doctors were slow to respond and make the proper diagnosis. Lacking treatment, the doctors administered palliatives and weekly vitamin B-12 injections.

Mary-Russell still managed to do some work in furtherance of Indian art, though at much lower levels than in her prime. She acted as a judge at the Hopi Craftsman Exhibition, but stopped making trips to the Hopi pueblos. She published her last article in 1953. It appeared in *Plateau* and was entitled "Art Department of the Museum of Northern Arizona."

Harold designed "a very functional two bedroom house, big enough but not too big for Mary-Russell to take care of," for the Sedona property. They constructed the home in 1950, and named it Red Ledge. Red Ledge included

MARY-RUSSELL AND HAROLD AT RED LEDGE, THEIR WINTER HOME
NEAR SEDONA, ARIZONA, 1951

quarters for Katharine Bartlett, who still lived with the Coltons and chauf-feured Harold and Mary-Russell back and forth between Sedona and Flagstaff. It also included a studio for Mary-Russell, which Harold encouraged her to use, hoping that she might regain her enthusiasm for art. The stimulus worked to a certain degree. Antoinette Jones, a neighbor, recalled those days "I enjoyed . . . watching the growth of the paintings that Mrs. Colton was doing in that little studio on the knoll."

Corky Jones wrote to Mary-Russell on January 9, 1952:

> *I'm so glad you are painting again, Mrs. Colton—how happy you must be at work again at it—and I'm anxious to see some of your paintings. I'm sure you'll feel better physically now that you are creating something.*

The effort to revive her interest in painting was short-lived, however. By the time Corky wrote her letter, Mary-Russell had painted her last work. It was done in the Sedona studio late in 1951, an oil entitled *Bell Rock and Courthouse Rock*. She also participated briefly in a new Flagstaff group, Northern Arizona Artists, which held an exhibition in July 1951. She entered one painting, *Sunset Lava Fields*, which had been done years earlier. She still enjoyed sketching, though, and would often amuse herself by drawing portraits in charcoal.

In 1952, Katharine's mother became ill and she went to the East Coast to take care of her. She was away for several weeks. On February 3, 1952, she wrote from Boston:

> *Dear Boss [her customary salutation on letters to Harold],*
>
> *I've been thinking a good deal these past two months that I have been staying with Mother for there was little else to do at times, and I have arrived at some long-thought-of decisions. I've been working for the Museum and living with you now for twenty-two years and loving it all, but what do I have to show for it? Most people of my age have families, homes and very responsible positions like vice-presidencies. I have a wonderful home with you but nothing to call my own. As I look back on it, the best years of my life have been wholly devoted to the Museum and to you and Mary-Russell, and especially the last years since the war when we have had no help. I have tried very hard to make*

things easier for you both in every way I could, and to do as many of the house-keeping chores as possible with my other work. In fact I often spend so much time on house keeping that I don't do the Museum work that I should, as you know. Now, also, when the Museum day is over, I need a change from thinking of Museum things. Living with it constantly, as we do, I find is becoming increasingly hard. I adore the Museum but I need to get away from it too.

All of which leads me to the thought that I would like to have a leave-of-absence from living with you, for a while until we see how it works out. Since you have been getting along without me for the past several months, and since you have Mrs. Shivers there at hand to help, this would seem a good time for me to make the break. If I can get along without you (perhaps I won't be able to) and you can get along without me, perhaps it will be permanent.

I want very much to have a home of my own and as soon as I can I would like to build on my Color Cove property. [Katharine had earlier purchased a lot next to the Coltons.] In the meantime I am going to live with Gene Foster in her house or some other nearby to Color Cove that we will rent. Page, her roommate, is going away in a few weeks.

I want you and Mary-Russell to know that I love you both dearly and nothing can ever change my affection and admiration for you both. I have loved living with you and being with you and doing all the things we have over the years, but I feel selfishly no doubt, that I need a change.

I shall see you every day & keep track of how you are, and will, of course, be on hand if you have any special need of me. While you are at Color Cove, I expect to work in the office every day and go to town with you on Tuesdays & Fridays as usual. If Mary-Russell wants me to stay with her any evening—if you have to go to meetings—I'll be glad to do so.

You both have been very wonderful to me—like a second family—for all the years I have lived with you, (which is more than I lived with my parents). I am not unmindful of my obligations and responsibilities toward you engen-dered by your long & close relationship, and therefore I want to have my house close to yours so I can be near you & do whatever I can when the need arises, which, after all, is occasionally and not all the time. I'd like to build a house this spring or summer if I can rake up the money.

I believe I can write this to you more clearly than I could tell you for I am not very good at speaking my thoughts. Moreover, I want to let you know now so you will have some time to make plans before my return. This has been a hard decision for me to make and a difficult letter to write. Please believe that my love for you both is very deep and sincere, and I don't want to hurt you, though I'm afraid I will with this letter. I think I'll be back around the 14th, by train, but will let you know more exactly later.

Very devotedly,
Katharine

The letter came as a shock, but Harold empathized with Katharine and sent her a generous and kindly reply:

My Dear Katharine,

I have been thinking over our situation here at home and remembering how you told me that you had been very unhappy during the summer. I realize that our mutual situation is a difficult one and I am anxious to arrange matters for the greatest happiness to us all.

I believe that the time has come when you would find more happiness in greater personal freedom than you can under our present domestic arrangement.

As the years pass Mary-Russell and I both realize, it is inevitable for us to desire to choose our own friends and be free to enjoy them; therefore, I do not feel our present financial arrangement is adequate to give you the personal freedom which I believe will bring you more happiness. I have placed in the budget of the Museum a sum raising your salary to cover board and lodging, when a change is made making you a "free woman," not subject to the whims of two elderly people. This will allow you to select your own surroundings, which we both feel is your natural right, you should desire.

You have been like a daughter to us and we will miss the close association, but if you were really our daughter, by this time you would want to be independent. A break like this should not destroy our warm and lasting friendship. You will always be like one of our family.

With love from us both.
I am affectionately
Harold S. Colton

Katharine moved out of Coyote Range in 1953, sharing a rental with Gene Foster until she was able to build her own home at 420 West Oak, only a couple of miles from the museum, which Gene then shared with her. Harold was able to absorb all of this and remain on friendly terms with Katharine, but Mary-Russell could not. Relations between Katharine and Mary-Russell had been cool for some time and Katharine's departure from the Colton home trig-gered outright hostility. Katharine wrote Harold, who was away in the East:

June 15, 1954

Dear Boss,

I have been going to see Mary-Russell every morning, and she seems to be getting along splendidly. Having the girls [granddaughters Robin and Denise] there each night is very good for her morale, and the girls seem to love it. . . .

I'm sorry that you are away this week, for we are having a pre-view and tea and exhibition of Gene's portraits. Viola Babbitt is having the tea at her house and has invited everybody in town. Gene will have 26 portraits—oils, charcoal drawings and terra cotta sculptures, which I wish you could see. I don't suppose Mary-Russell will come to the tea or the exhibition, later, and I shan't try to persuade her to. It makes me feel like a disinherited child to think that she won't come to my house to dinner or tea or lunch, and I suppose won't let you come either. There are so many times when I want to ask you, and yet I feel that I can't after the rebuff I received from her last summer, when I invited you to lunch and Suzanne too, and made it quite clear that Gene was working that day and wouldn't be there. I love you both so much, and I want you to come to see me. Maybe you and Suzanne would come for cocktails some afternoon, even if Mary-Russell won't. Gene is a very wonderful person, and so very talented and hard-working and courageous I wish you could know her as I do. She is very happy with her painting and all now and plans for the house. She often needs help on technical points of painting and Mary-Russell could give her so many pointers, I know, for there are no other artists in this area that know as well as she does. Ah, me, I didn't mean to go into all this, but I miss seeing you as much as I would like to.

The Sedona home did not meet expectations, especially without Katharine to act as chauffeur. Harold and Mary-Russell put it up for sale, and resumed their life at Coyote Range.

On the afternoon of August 22, 1953, the Museum of Northern Arizona celebrated its twenty-fifth birthday. Friends and supporters gathered and gave the Coltons a party. Mary-Russell attended, and to those who did not know her well, seemed to be in good condition. Harold noted that in spite of whatever problems she might be having in the privacy of their home, she was always able to make a good appearance during the few times that she could be coaxed to go out in public.

MARY-RUSSELL CONTINUED to make contributions to the museum. On December 27, 1954, she and Harold jointly made another gift of land to the Northern Arizona Society of Science and Art, an eleven-acre tract located west of the research center. She still worked on her beloved Hopi Craftsman Exhibition. As Harold wrote to a friend on July 6, 1955, "Mary-Russell and I are standing the strain of this four-day 4th of July celebration very well. We are about dead every night as we work from 9 to 6, but are spry the next morning."

At home, Mary-Russell's behavior was becoming a grave problem. At first she was merely forgetful, and began writing things down so that she would remember them. What seemed to be a normal consequence of aging progressed rapidly; she soon reached a point where she could not remember what she had said minutes earlier. At times, she would excuse her inability to remember where she had put things by blaming Harold, accusing him of hiding them from her. She became irritable and quarrelsome, and occasionally aggressive. Sufficiently self-aware to realize some of her problems, she began to suffer from depression.

Harold analyzed the situation in accordance with his training and his years as a scientist. He observed the facts and began writing notes to himself. At first, he seemed to think that Mary-Russell was simply behaving badly and that all she had to do was put her mind to the task of self-improvement.

MARY-RUSSELL WITH UWI KEWANWYTEWA,
SON OF JIMMY K., 1931

HAROLD BEGAN WINDING down his career as the director of the museum, devoting much effort to putting the institution that he and Mary-Russell had founded on a secure financial footing. He donated almost $180,000 ($900,000) worth of personal securities to the museum, and in 1952 his sister, Suzanne Wilson, and her son Richard gave the museum future oil and gas rights from wells in Texas that would in time produce $987,500. The gift was made in honor of Suzanne's recently deceased husband, and her son Robert Jr., who was killed in the WAR in 1944. Mary-Russell helped by making her final gifts of land to the museum, a ten-acre tract in 1955 and a twenty-six acre tract in 1957, bringing her total land contribution to one hundred-and-ten acres.

BEGINNING IN 1955, Mary-Russell turned more and more inward. She became testy, and the Coltons had trouble keeping servants because she was so hard on them with her complaining and fault-finding. They frequently consulted doctors, who continued giving her inconclusive tests. They were unable to suggest any remedies beyond vitamin B-12 shots and Phenobarbital, which failed to address the root cause.

Mary-Russell began to waken during the night with extreme stomach pains, which caused her to panic. The emotional distress exacerbated the stomach upset, setting up a vicious circle of cause and effect. It was difficult to calm her down, and often a doctor had to be called to administer a strong sedative. She was by now fearful of people, and extremely reluctant to leave Harold's side. In fact, she could seldom steel herself to leave Coyote Range.

Harold—knowing that his life was nearing its end—was trying mightily to conclude his many unfinished projects. He particularly wanted to publish some of his most significant work. More and more, however, Mary-Russell demanded that he give all his time to her.

The museum gave an exhibition of Mary-Russell's paintings in the fall of 1958. It included some of her last works, including those she painted in the studio at Color Cove. Mary-Russell attended the show, leading the public to believe that she was still functioning normally. The reality was that conditions at home were so difficult that Harold decided, coincident with the thirtieth anniversary of the founding of the museum, to resign as its director.

A party was given by friends and well-wishers on October 2, 1958 in observance of the museum's thirtieth anniversary. Museum employees contacted everyone they could think of and asked them to write letters for the anniversary celebration. The letters poured in—some two hundred fifty of them—and were bound into a book. They came from everywhere, the authors a *Who's Who* list in the arts and sciences in the Southwest, as well as relatives, friends, and townspeople. They were testimonials to the contributions that Harold and Mary-Russell made, and to their many kindnesses.

The staff led Harold and Mary-Russell to believe that the celebration was nothing more than a little buffet supper for insiders. When the Coltons arrived, they stepped into surprise party, a large gathering of friends, staff, and associates and the presentation of the bound volume of letters.

IN LATE 1958 Harold made note of Mary-Russell's past behavior, comparing it with her present conduct. Where she had been sweet and loving, she was nagging and suspicious. Where generous, selfish. Where she had liked a few people, she now disliked most people. Where she had been hospitable, she was now inhospitable. Where she had not been jealous, now she was. In addition he noted that she did not like to be alone, that she was forgetful, that she had fixations and that she sometimes unintentionally made false statements. He added: "Very nervous, with fits of depression, forgetful, sometimes forgets in a few minutes, lonely, timid."

In 1958, thinking to cheer her up, Harold searched through all of the available records and made a comprehensive catalog of all the paintings and sketches Mary-Russell had created during her lifetime. He prepared a separate page for each work, including a photograph wherever possible, along with the piece's statistics. He bound it in a leather notebook and gave it to her for Christmas.

MARY-RUSSELL AND HAROLD ARE HONORED AT A PARTY
CELEBRATING THE 30TH ANNIVERSARY OF THE MUSEUM OF
NORTHERN ARIZONA, 1958

ON JANUARY 1, 1959, Ned Danson replaced Harold as Director of the museum. By this time, Mary-Russell was experiencing active paranoia, which made her fearful and suspicious of others. She had a delusion that the change of directors was a takeover aimed at freezing her out of museum activities. This spurred her to write:

> Note, As the Museum of Northern Arizona (built on my donated property) has no longer any use for my personal services, I herewith tender my resignation as a member of the Museum of Northern Arizona. I also withdraw certain sums left in my will.

She then made an accounting of everything she had given to the museum over the years, going back to June 2, 1928. The list included items as small as $3.75 she spent for the Junior Art Show in 1934. The total was about $40,000 (a sum difficult to render in contemporary dollars because it consisted of a number of contributions over many years, but no doubt equal at least to $250,000).

A bright note occurred in July 1959 when Mary-Russell received a prestigious citation from the Indian Arts and Crafts Board. In it, Mary-Russell's essential qualities were clearly identified:

> United States
> Department Of The Interior
> Indian Arts and Crafts Board
> Washington 25, D. C.
>
> July 1, 1959
>
> Mary Russell-Ferrell Colton:
>
> You came from the East into a land which was new and strange to you. Soon you found a new life into which you fit yourself so naturally that you have become as one.
>
> Quietly you approached the Indian artist with the warmth of a friend and the humility of a learner, and he responded by giving generously of his culture. To this you added a depth of perception and artistic sensitivity which enabled you to measure his strengths and limitations.
>
> Realizing that this was expressive of a great tradition and part of our

national heritage, you exercised every effort to perpetuate this tradition so that generations yet to come might also enjoy it.

Yet this was never unthinking romanticism. In a practical sense you have demanded that the artist continually create, and strive towards ever-expanding goals. You have never allowed quality to be sacrificed for expediency.

You were never satisfied with merely learning of this culture. You made it your life work to share this with others, and to assist the Indian artist in every way possible. You established the Department of Art in the Museum of Northern Arizona as an important part of the program of that Institution. You developed many exhibitions which have become annual events, and are today so successful in the Museum's activities.

You gave great assistance to the Indian Arts and Crafts Board in the first years of its organization, and you have been of continuing inspiration in the carrying out of its work.

Rarely does a non-Indian have the opportunity to establish an Indian tradition. Yet, in 1938, you proposed a development in Hopi silversmithing which had a long, slow genesis. Today that style of silverwork has become familiar, and is popularly regarded as representing a traditional craft expression of these people. But you were careful not to dictate; yours was the role of counselor—in truth, a pupil turned teacher.

In recognition of what you have so unselfishly given of yourself for the betterment of others, the Indian Arts and Crafts Board takes pride and pleasure in presenting you with this Certificate of Appreciation.

René d'Harnoncourt
Chairman

Mary-Russell replied to d'Harnoncourt:

I wish to express my sincere appreciation of your kind letter.

It is, indeed, a happy thing to feel that others are aware of the work which we have carried on for so many years. I am very proud of my Certificate from the Indian Arts and Crafts Board of the Department of the Interior.

My only worry now is to find a young woman to train to take up my position and carry on the work among our Indian peoples.

Dr. Colton joins me in sincere good wishes and the hope that you will come our way soon again.

This was Mary-Russell's last hurrah. Her condition deteriorated ever more rapidly, and she began showing clear signs of confusion. Her behavior was sometimes bizarre.

By 1961, Mary-Russell had stopped writing to her old friends, which was quite a departure from the norm, as she had always been considerate and prolific with her correspondence. In February 1961, Harold wrote Blanche Shaw Blocklinger, "I am writing to you for Mary-Russell who scarcely ever writes a letter now, at least she puts them off and forgets."

He amplified his comments in a letter to Blanche in May 1961:

It is almost impossible for me to get away anywhere at present because I cannot leave Mary-Russell as I have no one to take care of her and she will not go anywhere except short day trips about the country, particularly the Painted Desert area. She does not paint anymore so is at loose ends most of the time. Physically she is pretty well but very forgetful.

ALTHOUGH QUITE ILL BY THIS TIME, MARY-RUSSELL IS STILL ABLE TO ACT AS A JUDGE AT THE HOPI CRAFTSMAN EXHIBITION, 1959.

The year 1962 was the turning point in Mary-Russell's life, ending her role as a functional adult. The year began badly. Harold noted in his day book that on January 14, Mary-Russell was suffering sciatic pains. On January 16, she fell and injured her coccyx, which caused considerable suffering. Dr. Kahle attended her, giving her shots of ACTH, a powerful steroid, on January 16, 20, and 26. The doctor was concerned that she might have fractured her coccyx, so he x-rayed her on January 29. Fortunately, there was no break, and eventually the wound healed.

She became restless, irritable, and demanding—even abusive—to Harold. There were days when she would walk from the house to Harold's office twenty yards away, tell him something, and return to the house, only to repeat the performance a few minutes later, telling him the same thing, with no memory of the previous visit. This was observed to happen as often as thirty times a day. On April 7, she attended her last meeting of the Board of Trustees of the Northern Arizona Society of Science and Art.

Harold tried desperately to find some way to comfort her. The only thing that worked was to take her for a drive in the country to visit some of the places that she loved. Harold's eyesight was poor, so he had one of the employees drive them. He made notes of the trips in his day book for 1962:

March 15 trip to Grand Falls, March 17 trip to Page, March 18 trip to Mormon Lake, March 25 trip to Grand Canyon, March 31 trip to Verde Valley, April 1 trip to Allan Lake in the morning, Kendrick Park in the afternoon, April 5 trip to Oraibi, April 12 trip to Petrified Forest, April 14 trip around the San Francisco Peaks, April 15 trip to Parks, April 19 trip to Mingus Mountain, April 21 trip to Tuba City, April 29 trip to Wupatki and Sunset Crater, May 3 trip to Crack-in-Rock, May 10 trip to Grass Tank, May 12 trip to Stoneman Lake, May 19 trip to Wupatki, May 20 trip to Sedona.

These drives calmed Mary-Russell, but they took up so much of Harold's time that he found it impossible to get any work done.

On May 23, 1962, Mary-Russell and Harold observed their golden wedding anniversary. As with all things in their lives, this was done quietly and without ostentation. They were driven to the Grand Canyon, where they had lunch at El Tovar, then returned to Coyote Range. That evening Ferrell,

Denise, and a friend came over for supper. Later in the evening, Ned and Jessica Danson paid a visit.

After the golden wedding observance, the day trips to pacify Mary-Russell resumed:

> *May 27 trip to Upper Lake Mary in the morning and to the Cinder Hills in the afternoon, May 31 trip to the Cinder Hills, June 7 trip to Merriam Crater, June 10 trip to Lake Mary, June 16 trip to Cinder Hills, June 23 trip to Cinder Hills.*

When it was time for the Hopi Craftsman Exhibition in 1962, Mary-Russell was in no condition to contribute to it. All the decisions had to be made by Harold, who was beginning to give way under the strain. As he wrote later:

> *My old age seemed to strike in the summer of 1962. I had been pretty well all spring, notwithstanding Mary-Russell's nagging and occasional belligerent attacks when she would, if I disagreed with her, hit me or slap me, often knocking off my glasses. Once she kicked me in the seat of my pants. As she did not wear pointed shoes, it did not amount to anything more than my walking out the front door and going to my office with injured feelings.*

On June 29, 1962 Harold noted in his day book, "Headache, Dr. Sitterley, Tension." Harold's illness worsened, forcing him to spend many days in bed. A nurse was hired to give him home care. He wrote that "Mary-Russell was very upset by the nurse in my bedroom and punched and poked her around. The nurse was actually afraid of her and left."

On July 9, Dr. Currin diagnosed Harold's problem as a stroke. He was not able to get out of bed even to eat dinner until July 22. A second nurse, Ruth Hixson, was hired. She too was attacked by Mary-Russell but was tough enough to stay on the job and tend to Harold.

On August 7, Harold had an appointment at Dr. Currin's office. Here, away from Mary-Russell's hearing, the doctor told him that she must be hospitalized. Harold—driven beyond his breaking point—reluctantly agreed.

As he explained in his autobiography, getting Mary-Russell to the hospital did not go smoothly. "On August 8th, an attempt was made to take her to Phoenix. This failed as she refused to get in the car."

Finally the climactic event, the last episode of Mary-Russell's life in Flagstaff, occurred. Harold described it in his autobiography:

On Sunday, August 12, 1962, Mary-Russell made arrangements with our maintenance man to take her for a ride around 10 o'clock. Before she left she came to my office where Ferrell and I were discussing some business matters. She did not agree with our decisions and picked up a paper weight and started to hit me with it. Ferrell tried to stop her and she turned on him. As Ferrell was not too well at the time, he collapsed. Mary-Russell left and went for her ride. I was able to get hold of a doctor who called an ambulance, and Ferrell was taken to the Flagstaff Hospital. [Ferrell's recollection is that he was not present when the quarrel broke out but was called to the scene by his father while it was in progress.]

At first it was thought that Ferrell had had a heart attack, but later it was diagnosed as shock. Dr. Currin was called and it was decided that Mary-Russell should be taken to Camelback Hospital in Phoenix, at once.

It was a great blow to me to have her go. Of course she was unwilling, but with sedation she was taken to Phoenix.

Harold called Dr. Currin and Dr. George Yard, both of whom agreed that Mary-Russell should be taken to the hospital in Phoenix immediately. Because this incident occurred on a Sunday, it was difficult to make the necessary arrangements. The only ambulance they could find belonged to the Flagstaff Mortuary. Dr. Currin came to Coyote Range and injected Mary-Russell with a sedative and she was placed in the ambulance; John Warren of the mortuary drove her to Phoenix. Ned Danson and nurse Ruth Hixson went along. Danson said later, "It was the worst thing I ever had to do in my life."

The strain of this traumatic parting with Mary-Russell caused Harold to have another stroke on August 15, this one so severe that he was hospitalized.

As soon as Harold was on his feet again, he inquired after Mary-Russell's health, but was not allowed to see her. He wrote, "I was told by the doctor not to see her as it would cause so much emotion that it would injure both of us. Christmas, 1962, was the first Christmas that we were separated in 50 years."

MARY-RUSSELL MADE two attempts to write to Harold soon after she was hospitalized, the handwriting clearly showing her loss of control. The first one read: "Dear Harold. [illegible]. I have received yellow roses. [Three or four illegible words]. Hope to be home soon. Love you."

The second letter was dated August 17, 1962. The top part is written by Mary-Russell in a barely legible scrawl.

Have received four [flowers] lots of fun, hurry up and come. Fine weather and so many interesting things to do. Much love and please hurry dear. We are sitting in the [illegible] and the weather is very warm. We miss Tawa [their dog]. Please keep him well. Love, for mother soon.

On the rest of the note paper there is a message from Kathryn Lines, one of the nurses assigned to Mary-Russell:

Mrs. Colton is still disoriented tho she is quite cheerful. Is anxious to be home, of course. I am her special nurse for a few days until she becomes a little more settled. We are taking good care of Mrs. Colton & she is hoping to join you before long.

The hope that Mary-Russell could return home was unrealized. Even though she had her moments of lucidity at first, she soon lost ground, and in a few weeks had almost entirely forgotten her former life. She was no longer able to write.

Still shaky from his two strokes, Harold was invited to Tucson, where his sister Suzanne lived on a ranch. He seemed to tolerate the trip well at first, but soon became violently ill, and was rushed to the hospital where it was found that he had pneumonia. He rallied, and on October 31, he was able to write of Mary-Russell's fate to two of her dearest friends from the past, Isabel Cartwright and Blanche Blocklinger (the former Blanche Shaw). Both Isabel and Blanche responded and kept in touch with Harold through Christmas cards and other correspondence.

Harold gradually reduced the frequency of his letters to Mary-Russell, but never failed to send her flowers and cards for special occasions such as her birthday, Valentine's Day, and the like. In time, he and Ferrell were allowed to visit her, which they did regularly. She did not recognize them. She could not remember any recent events, but sometimes had a dim recall of pleasant events of the past. The things she remembered most were childhood days on her "Paradise," Broadwater Island.

Mary-Russell had around-the-clock care, with three nurses working eight-hour shifts. Hazel Livingston became Mary-Russell's primary nurse and took care of her for several years. Harold corresponded with Nurse Livingston frequently. After a short time, Mary-Russell was moved from Camelback to an outcare facility called The Bells Lodge, where she spent the rest of her life. Her health was generally good, though she fell in her room and broke her hip in May 1965.

On December 14, 1967, Ms. Livingston wrote:

> *Mrs. Colton is doing fine. Was amused at her yesterday. After her bath I said, "My Mary R. you look so pretty." She smiled & said, "Do you really think so." Thrilled me to death to hear her speak out a full sentence. She don't speak often and only a word or two. At least she knows she is getting attention which she loves.*

MARY-RUSSELL IN HER ROOM AT HER NURSING HOME, BELLS LODGE, IN PHOENIX, 1970. ONE OF HER PAINTINGS HANGS ABOVE HER.

By this time, Mary-Russell was barely able to feed herself. Her physical and mental functions were steadily declining.

Relieved of the burden of trying to cope with Mary-Russell's illness at home, Harold had a final burst of activity in his own life, and was able to turn his attention to the completion of unfinished projects. One of these was Mary-Russell's decades-long work on Hopi dyes, for which she had compiled many notes, recipes, and a partial manuscript. Harold applied the finishing touches to her work and published *Hopi Dyes* in 1965. It is still recognized as the leading authority on the subject.

Harold Colton died, still a resident of Coyote Range, on December 29, 1970, at age 89. His remains were cremated. Ferrell took the ashes to Philadelphia and buried them in the family plot.

Mary-Russell Ferrell Colton survived her beloved husband by only seven months, passing away at The Bells Lodge in Phoenix on July 16, 1971, at the age of 82.

During a lucid moment before she was hospitalized, she wrote her thoughts about her death:

To my husband and to those others that are dear to me,

The following directions embody my wishes, as to the final arrangements for my mortal body when I no longer have need of it upon this earth.

It is my wish that my body shall be cremated and the ashes preserved by my family, until such time as those of my husband may be mingled with mine, when they both shall be committed to the winds of heaven. It is desired that the ashes be released from a plane over the cedar country, on the Painted Desert, east of the Peaks.

I request that my body shall not be embalmed unless absolutely necessary.

No one shall look upon my face when the spirit has left the body other than my husband and my son, for remember that you shall not find one there.

Other than these directions I shall wish my family to arrange everything in the simplest and least painful manner for those I shall leave behind.

If they wish I would suggest a quiet Episcopal service in our home, for relatives and friends. The casket shall not be viewed.

As I do not feel that this should be a sorrowful occasion for I have known great happiness but only a temporary parting, I should like to have the 23rd Psalm, carrying its message of Peace and hope, close the service for me.

Perhaps she never made these wishes known. She was cremated but her ashes were not scattered over the Painted Desert. Instead they were preserved and Ferrell and his second wife Lita took them to Philadelphia in an urn for burial.

Harold and Mary-Russell lie side-by-side in the Colton family plot in the West Laurel Hills Cemetery outside Philadelphia. Their graves are marked by a single tombstone which simply records their names and dates of birth and death. Below Harold's statistics appears the single word, "Scientist," and below Mary-Russell's the single word, "Artist."

APPENDICES

Appendix A: List of Artwork by Mary-Russell Ferrell Colton

COMPILED BY HAROLD COLTON as a Christmas present for Mary-Russell in 1958. (Some dates—not given by Harold—are estimated.)

"Pre-1910"	*Self-portrait*, oil
"Pre-1911"	*Portrait of Julia McMahon*, charcoal
1901	*Mother Rabbit with Young*, watercolor
1905	*Lobster, a still life*, medium unknown (her first sale)
1908	*White Bowl*, watercolor
	Still Life, watercolor
1910	*Lady in Black*, oil
	In the Selkirk Mountains, medium unknown
	The Tarn, Selkirk Mountains, oil
1911	*Rocks in Maine Coast*, watercolor
1913	*Mt. Sir Donald*, oil
	Church at Ranchos de Taos, watercolor
	Grand Canyon, oil
	Zuni Corn Mountains, oil
1914	*Walpi*, oil
1918	*Navajo Girl and Goat*, oil
"1913-20"	*Canyon de Chelly*, oil

Navajos in Canyon de Chelly, oil

Ancient Pecos Church, watercolor

Hart Prairie, oil

Fish Wharf, medium unknown

Rocks and Surf on Cranberry, medium unknown

"1914-20" *Ferrell as a baby,* oil

"1920s" *Peonies,* watercolor

Contemporary Mural, charcoal

Clouds Over Cedars, oil

Hohokam Moon, oil

Study of Little Boy in Studio (Ferrell and Gyp), oil

Hopi Kiva, oil

Valley of the Little Colorado, oil

1920 *Painted Desert from Interior Valley,* oil

Grandmother's Garden, portraits of Ferrell and Sabin, oil

Havasupai, watercolor

Schooner in Fog, oil

1921 *Out On the Reservation,* watercolor

Autumn in the Studio, watercolor

1922 *Sunrise on the Painted Desert from Crater's Mouth,*
watercolor

Sunrise in the Aspens, watercolor

Island Pastures, watercolor

1923 *Desert Range Near Tucson,* oil

Valley of the Gods, oil

1925 *Red Rock Country (Court House Rock),* oil

Canyon Glow, oil

Afternoon Sandstorm in Painted Desert, oil

Across the Wepo Wash, oil

Gray Veils of Evening, oil

1926 *California Valley,* oil

Rest on the Little Colorado—horses, oil

Mishongnovi and *Shipaulovi* (two panels), oil

	Senator Hochderffer's House "Summit Ranch," oil
	Golden Hour, oil
	Little Colorado Valley from Cedars, oil
	A Study of Textures, Red Phlox, oil
	Flower Study, oil
1928	*Rock of Walpi,* oil
1929	*Cloud Fountains,* oil
	San Francisco Peaks, oil
"1930s"	*San Francisco Peaks from Sunset Lava,* oil
	Cinder Hills, Sunset Crater National Monument, oil
	Golden Aspens, oil
	Navajo Family, oil
	Sheep in Cedars, oil
	Portrait of Lucile Jeager, oil
	Thelma, oil
	Sunset Lava Flow, oil
	Aspens in Fall, oil,
	Old Junipers, oil,
	Valley of the Painted Hills, oil,
	Valley of the Little Colorado, oil
	Aspens, with Humphreys Peak in the background, oil
	Landscape, oil
1930	*Sunrise on Aspen Slopes,* watercolor
	Red Rock Country, oil
	Sunset Crater, oil
1931	*Little Painted Hills,* oil
	Sequaptewa, Weaver of Hotevilla, oil
1933	*Ferrell and Gyp,* oil
1934	*Hopi Weaver,* pen and ink
1935	*The Squall, Road in Kauai,* oil 1935
	Slopes of Haleakala, oil
1938	*Penang, Barge and Stevedores,* oil
1939	*Lonesome Hole,* oil

Autumn Patterns, Arizona (Schultz Creek Canyon), oil 1939

Balinese Dancers, oil

Balinese Woman, oil

1942   *Edmund Nequatewa*, gesso and oil

1950   *Navajo Man and Woman*, charcoal

1951   *Bell Rock & Court House*, oil

Appendix B: Mary-Russell's Paintings in Exhibitions of The Ten

Year	Painting
1917	*Navajo Shepherdess*
	Hohokam Moon
	The Silver Dawn
	A Drowsy Afternoon in Walpi, Arizona
	Old Church, Laguna, N. Mexico
	The Spanish Patio
	California Building, San Diego Exposition
	Yosemite Valley
	Walpi Pueblo
	Three Hopi Maidens
	Morning Cook Fires, Taos
	A Court in Taos
	Ancient Pecos Mission, New Mexico
	Dawn, Oak Creek Canyon, Arizona
	Evening in the Canyon, Arizona
	Quaking Aspens
1921	*Out on the Hopi Mesas*
	A Greeting to the Dawn
	The Desert's Secret
	Dream Canyon, Arizona
	Riders of the Painted Desert

1924   *The Home of the Ancient Ones, Painted Desert*
The Place of the Gods
Evening Glow, Southern Arizona
Cinder Cone and San Francisco Peaks
Approach of Night, Painted Desert
Desert Rain, Arizona
The Glorious Moment

1925   *Desert Range*
Rock of Walpi
Gray Veils of Evening
Red Rock Country
Children of the Mesa
Oraibi Mesa
Sunrise
Aspen Country

1926   *Afternoon Sandstorm: Painted Desert*
A Rest by the Little Colorado
Valley of the Little Colorado
Afternoon Across the Weapo Wash
Canyon Glow

1927   *The Dryad's Knoll*
The Golden Hour
Embroideries of Gold
Echo Cliffs
Sunset and Moonglow

1928   *Spring in the High Pasture*
Fall and the Shower of Gold
The Pals Consent to Pose—Ferrell & Gyp
Cloud Fountain
Turquoise and Gold
A California Valley
In the Valley of the Painted Hills

Old Pecos Church
Desert Shadows

1929   Primitive Enigma
Tropic Waters
Arizona Mountain Flowers
Golden Hour
Cloud Fountains
The Lonesome Hole
San Francisco Peaks
Rock of Walpi
Sunset: Lava Field
A Sketch: Juliet
The Cinder Hills

1930   The Lonesome Hole
Sunset Lava Field
Valley of the Painted Hills
A California Valley
The Golden Hour

1931   Cinder Hills
A California Valley
Sunset Crater and Lava Flow
Hopi Indian Spinner: Sequaptewa
Arizona Wild Flowers

1933   Hawaiian Coast
Pali Cliffs, Oahu
Rain in the Jungle, Kauai
The Squall, Kauai
The Plantation, Oahu
Cocoanut Palms, Honolulu
Fishing Sampans
Honolulu Harbor from the Hills

1936   *Arizona Dawn*
           The Golden Hour
           Cinder Hills
           Arizona Wild Flowers
           Rock of Walpi

1937   *Hopi Interpreter*
           Hopi Girl
           Rock of Walpi

1939   *Autumn Patterns, Arizona*
           A Balinese Woman
           The Squall—Kauai
           Dawn Glow, Arizona
           Dressing for the Dance, Bali

1940   *Autumn Patterns, Arizona*
           Dressing for the Dance, Bali
           Dawn Glow, Arizona

Mary-Russell's Gifts of Land

TO THE MUSEUM OF NORTHERN ARIZONA

Section 4, Township 21 North, Range 7 East

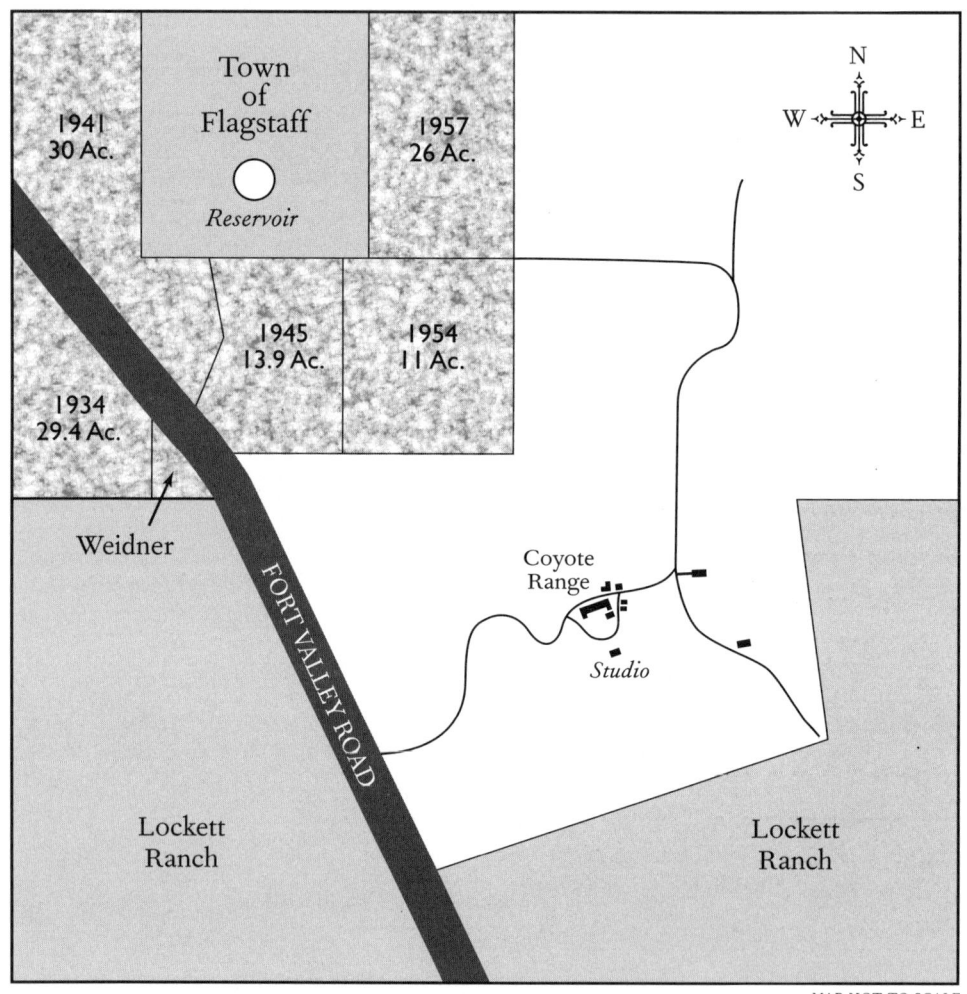

Town
of
Flagstaff

Reservoir

1941
30 Ac.

1957
26 Ac.

1945
13.9 Ac.

1954
11 Ac.

1934
29.4 Ac.

Weidner

FORT VALLEY ROAD

Coyote
Range

Studio

Lockett
Ranch

Lockett
Ranch

N
W — E
S

MAP NOT TO SCALE

Lands given to the Museum of Northern Arizona by Mary-Russell Ferrell Colton.

BIBLIOGRAPHY

Books

Ashworth, Donna. *Biography of a Small Mountain.* Flagstaff, Arizona: Small
    Mountain Books, 1991.

Cline, Platt. *Mountain Town.* Flagstaff, Arizona: Northland Publishing, 1994.

Colton, Mary-Russell F. *Art for the Schools of the Southwest: An Outline for the
    Public and Indian Schools.* Museum of Northern Arizona Bulletin 6.
    Flagstaff, Arizona, 1934.

————. *Hopi Dyes.* Flagstaff, Arizona: Museum of Northern Arizona, 1965.

Elliott, Melinda. *Great Excavations, Tales of Early Southwestern Archaeology,
    1888-1939.* Santa Fe, New Mexico: School of American Research
    Press, 1995.

Jones, Courtney R. *Letters From Wupatki.* Tucson: University of Arizona
    Press, 1995.

Miller, Jimmy H. *The Life of Harold Sellers Colton, A Philadelphia Brahmin in
    Flagstaff.* Tsaile, Arizona: Navajo Community College Press, 1991.

Nequatewa, Edmund. *Truth of the Hopi and Other Clan Stories.* Museum of
    Northern Arizona Bulletin 8. Flagstaff, Arizona, 1936.

Putnam, William. *The Great Glacier and Its House.* New York: American Alpine
    Club, 1982.

Smith, Watson. *The Story of the Museum of Northern Arizona.* Flagstaff,
    Arizona: Museum of Northern Arizona, 1969.

Stricker, Michele Pavone & Sydney, Patricia Tanis. *Fern I. Coppedge, A Forgotten Woman*. Doylestown, Pennsylvania: James A. Michener Arts Center, 1990.

Whiting, Alfred F. *Ethnobotany of the Hopi*. Museum of Northern Arizona Bulletin 10. Flagstaff, Arizona, 1939.

Magazines

Museum Notes, Publication of the Museum of Northern Arizona, Flagstaff. This was published quarterly from 1928 until 1939, when its name was changed to Plateau. All issues.

Plateau, Publication of the Museum of Northern Arizona, Flagstaff. All issues from 1939 through 1971.

Mangum, Richard and Sherry. "The Hopi Silver project of the Museum of Northern Arizona," *Plateau*, n. s., 56, no. 1 (1995).

————. "Brush Strokes on the Plateau," *Plateau* 56, no. 1 (1984): pp. 22–23.

Newspapers

Coconino Sun, Flagstaff, Arizona. All issues from 1926 through 1962.

Archival Materials

The archives of the Museum of Northern Arizona contain a Colton vault in which the family records are kept. These files begin with the designation MS 207.

Records of Coconino County, Arizona, contained in the office of the Coconino County Recorder. The authors searched the Deed indexes and books.

Records of Coconino County, Arizona contained in the office of the Clerk of the Superior Court for Probate information.

Index

Page numbers in italics refer to images.

RICHARD K. MANGUM is a native of Flagstaff, Arizona, and a life-long resident. After graduating from Flagstaff High School in 1954, he attended the
University of Arizona where he received a B. A. degree in English and a J. D.
degree in Law. He was employed in the general practice of law in Flagstaff
from 1961 until 1976, when he became a Judge of the Superior Court of
Coconino County, a position he held until 1993, when he retired. He then
changed careers, to live his dream of becoming a writer. Since then he and
Sherry have written and published four books. He is President Emeritus of the
Arizona Historical Society, Northern Division, and Historian-in-Residence at
the Museum of Northern Arizona.

SHERRY G. MANGUM moved to Flagstaff when she was seven years old
and feels almost like a native. She is a professional photographer, specializ-
ing in local landscapes. She is an Historian-in-Residence at the Museum of
Northern Arizona and the director of the Oral History program of the
Flagstaff/Coconino County Public Library. She and Richard are avid hikers.
Two of their books are hiking guides to the region.